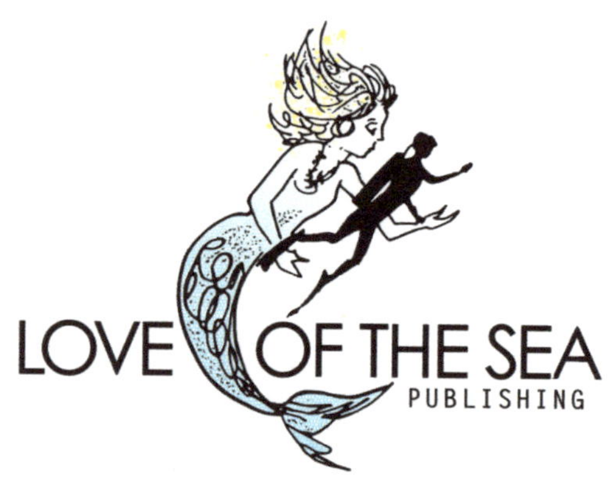

Paintings and words by Dominique Serafini

Published by Love of the Sea Publishing

Photos from my personal collection and from my friends Dominique Arrieu, Kamel Benabid, Yves Coutisson, Norbert Genetiaux, Luc Gilbert de Fontaine, Santi Patel, Catherine Salisbury, Sonia Semenic and Emmanuel Tosi.

Thank you to Catherine Salisbury, Jean-Michel Cousteau, Nicolas Barraqué and my diver friends who have accompanied me underwater all of these years.

Painting My Life in Blue
ISBN : 978-1-990238-97-0

Travels Into the Blue

It is forbidden to forbid to dream.

It was Paris, May 1968. I was at the National School of Fine Arts. I was 22 years old and was driven by the passion in my heart. I wanted to leave the grey urban milieu of my childhood and paint my world blue. With my pencils and paint brushes as my only weapons, I set off to pursue my dream: to join the Cousteau team, to paint, to dive and to sail the seas.

Many years later, off the island of Martinique, Cousteau's boat, the Calypso, anchored in front of my house and I became a member of the Cousteau team. I lived my dream. Sketch pads in hand, I boarded the Calypso to create 17 graphic novels for children. This 'bande dessinée' series called « l'Aventure de l'équipe Cousteau en bandes dessinées » was my life work. It was 20 years of pure happiness thanks to Jacques-Yves Cousteau.

After Captain Cousteau's death, I took to the sea on my sailboat and continued my life, diving and painting the beauty of the underwater world and stopping in far-away places.

Through my paintings, I invite you too to travel into blue.

Dominique Serafini

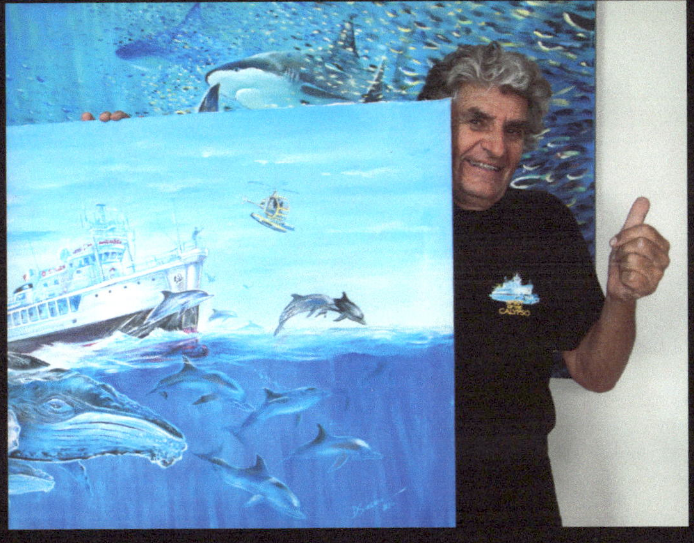

DOMINIQUE SERAFINI

Painter-illustrator born in Paris in 1946, Dominique Serafini graduated from the l'École Nationale des Beaux-Arts. His paintings and illustrations of life underwater can be seen around the world. On board the legendary Calypso, he created the graphic novel series called «L'aventure de l'équipe Cousteau en bandes dessinées».

He has written several other books, most notably «DreamWrecks» with Cathy Salisbury which later became a television series. Recently he created a graphic novel about the shipwrecks of Saint-Pierre in Martinique called «Shipwrecks of the Volcano».

He has continued his work as an artist-ecologist and has published books on whales, orcas and ocean plastics.

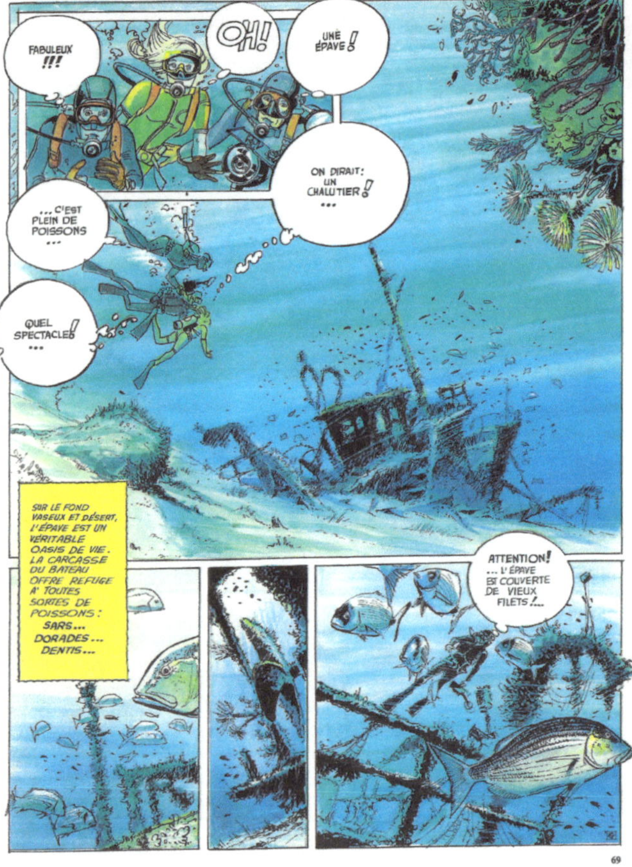

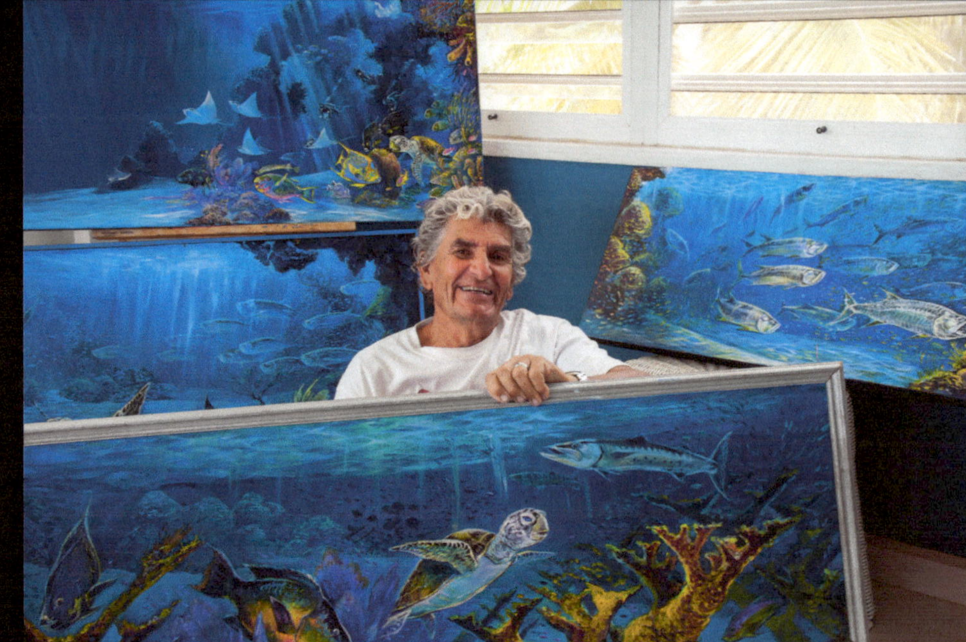

The 1970s... my first fin kicks and drawings in the dive magazines of the time in France: « l'Aventure Sous-Marine» as well as « Océans ». An idea came to me while I was living in Cassis... a beginner's guide to diving. «La Plongée Sous-Marine avec Rodolfo Betti» was first published serially in « Océans » and then in Italian in «Mondo Sommerso ». After, it was translated in Spanish, German and English. With this first success I would pursue Cousteau with my idea of a series of graphic novels about the Odyssey of the Calypso.

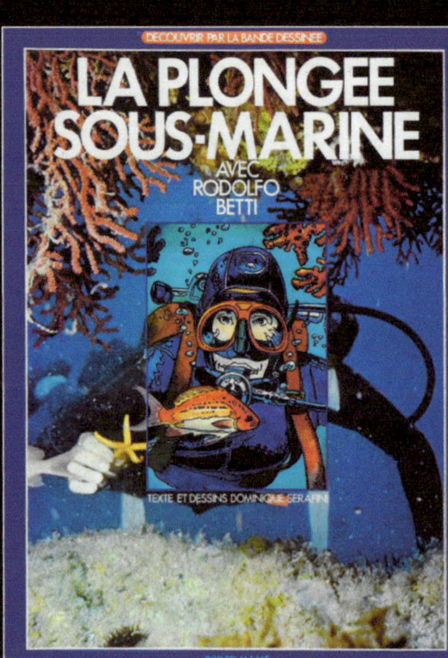

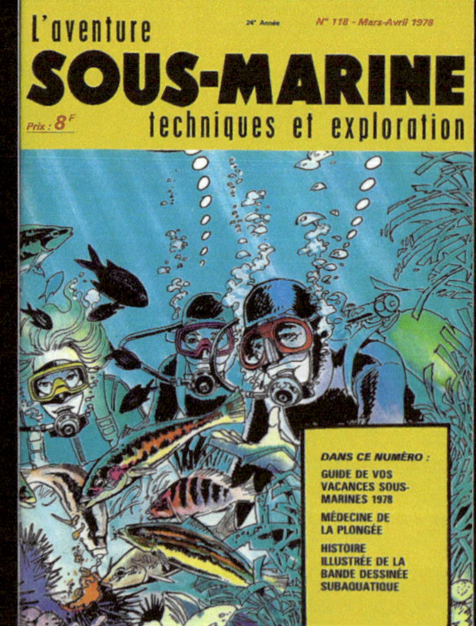

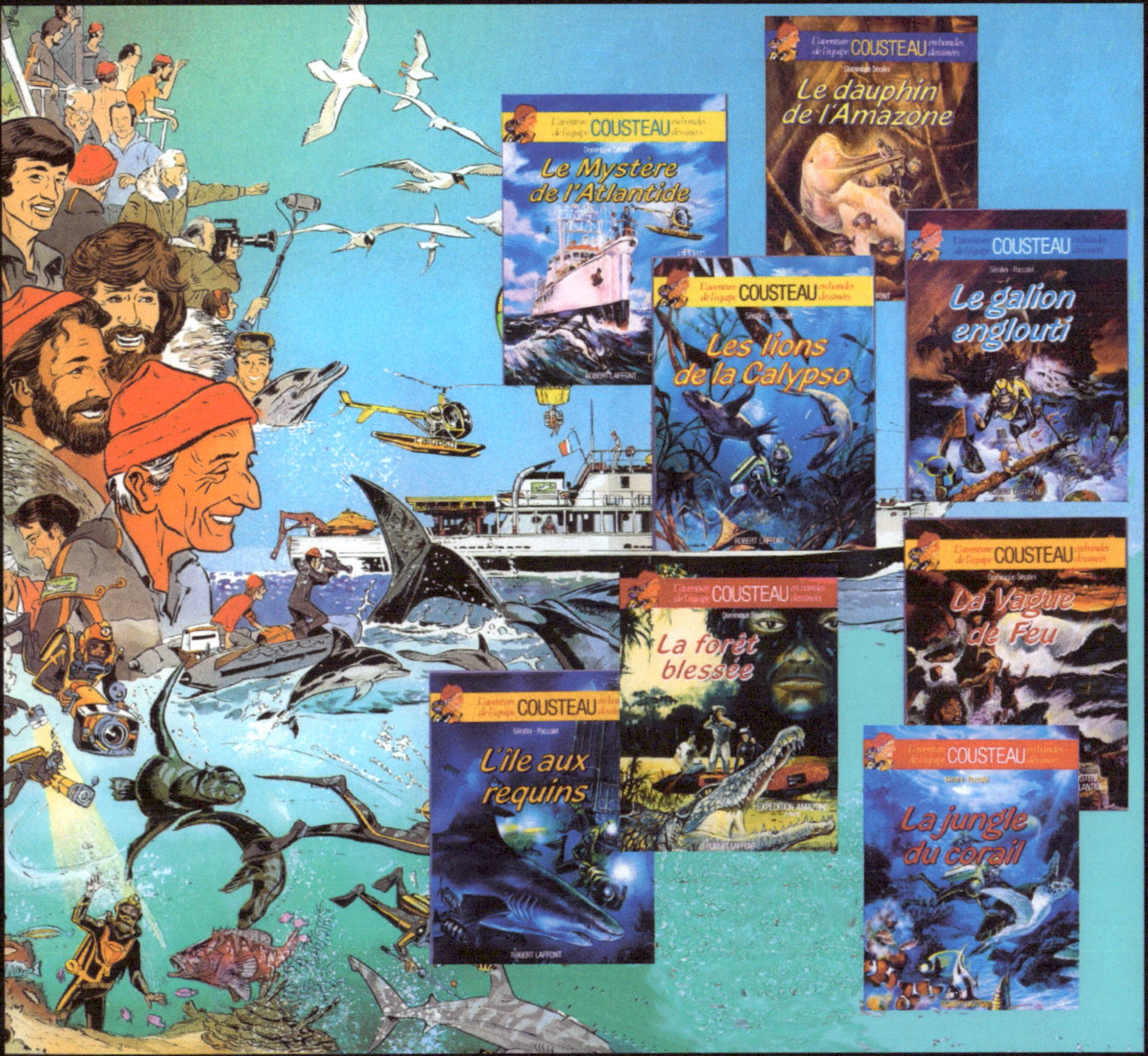

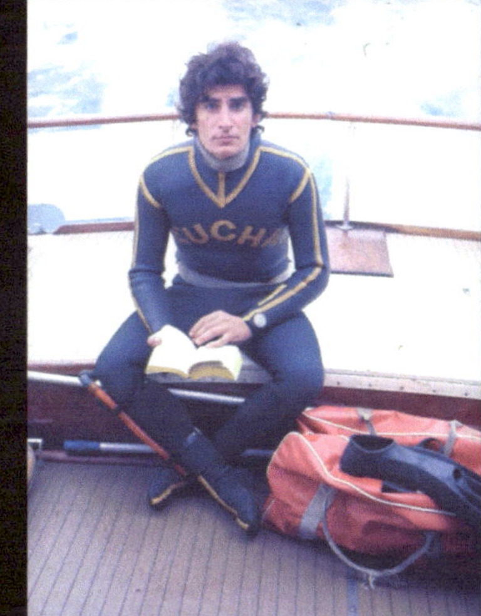

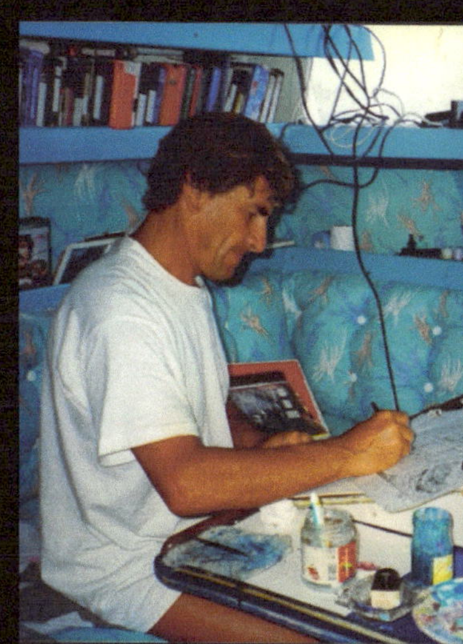

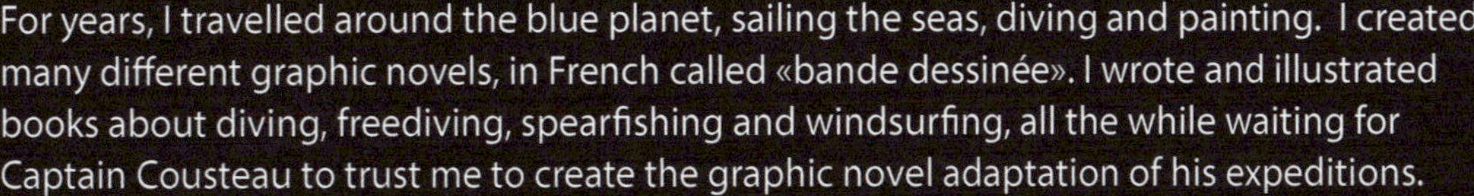

For years, I travelled around the blue planet, sailing the seas, diving and painting. I created many different graphic novels, in French called «bande dessinée». I wrote and illustrated books about diving, freediving, spearfishing and windsurfing, all the while waiting for Captain Cousteau to trust me to create the graphic novel adaptation of his expeditions.

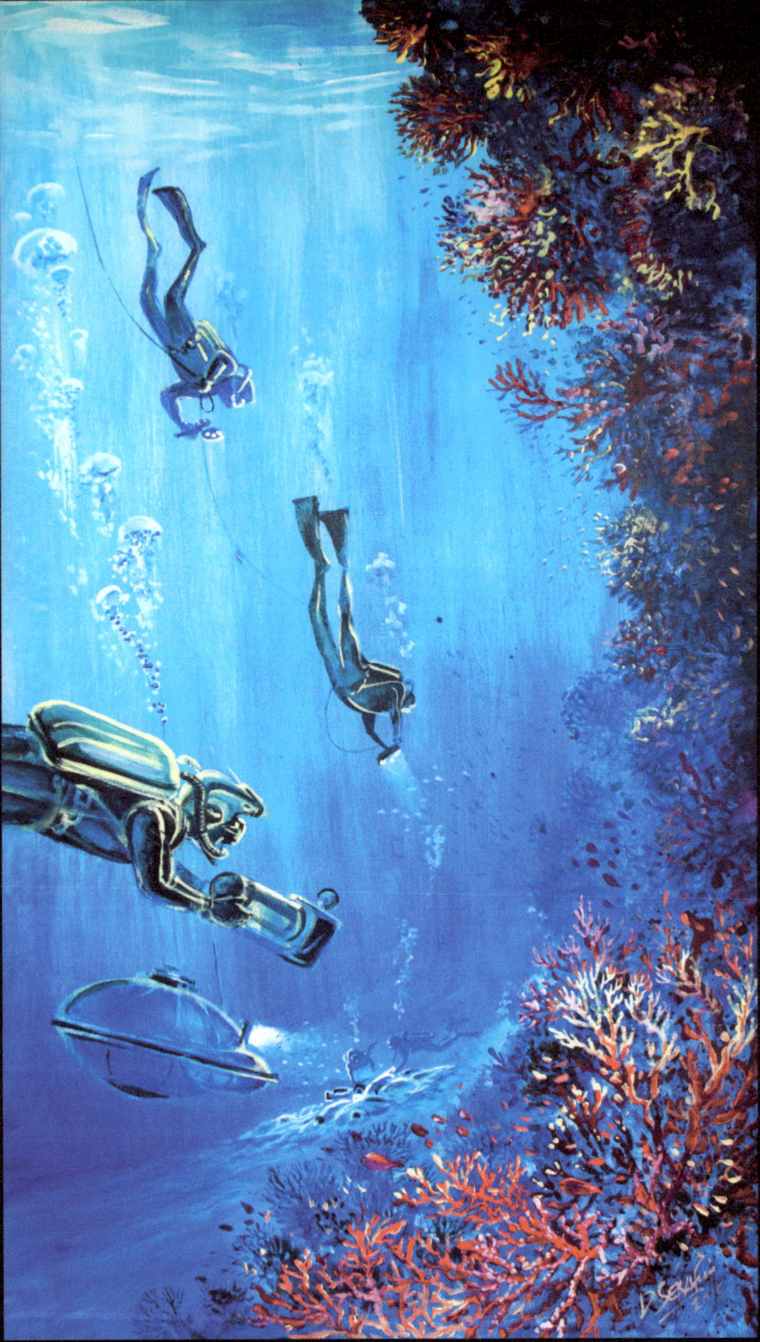

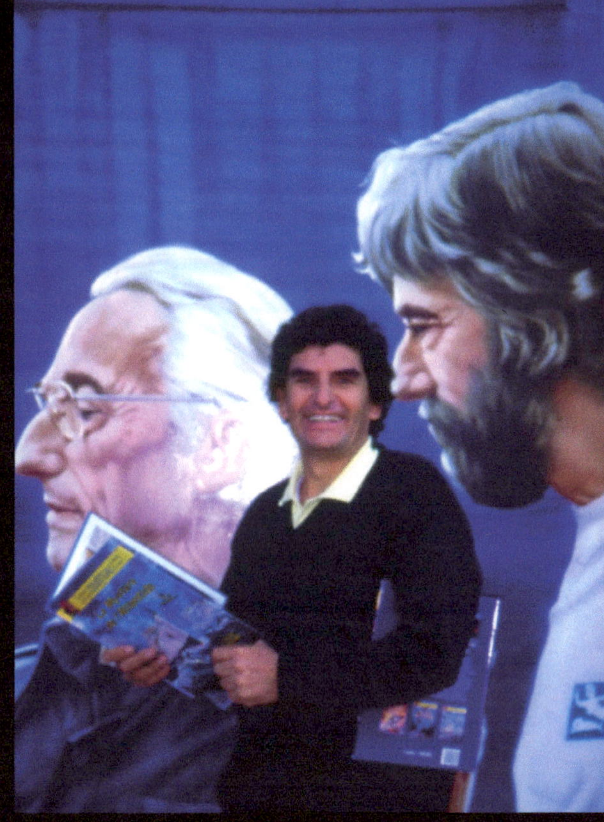

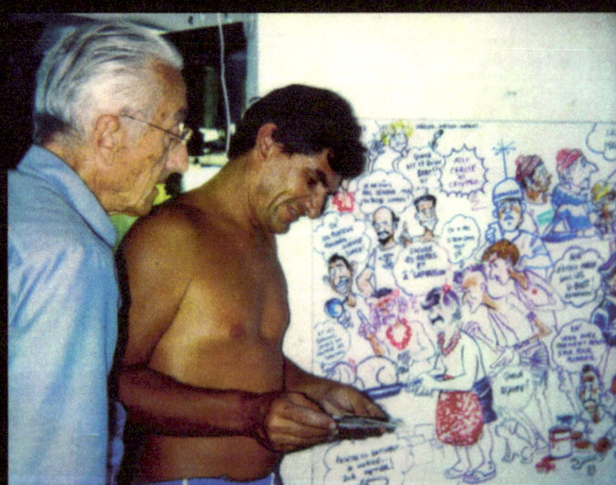

I wanted to dive with Albert Falco, paint on board the Calypso and share ideas with Jacques-Yves and Jean-Michel Cousteau. The members of the Cousteau team became the characters for my book series.

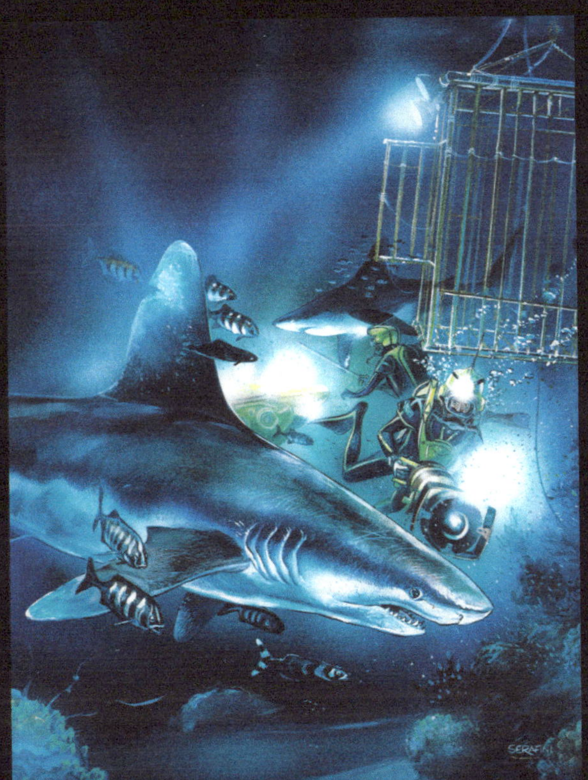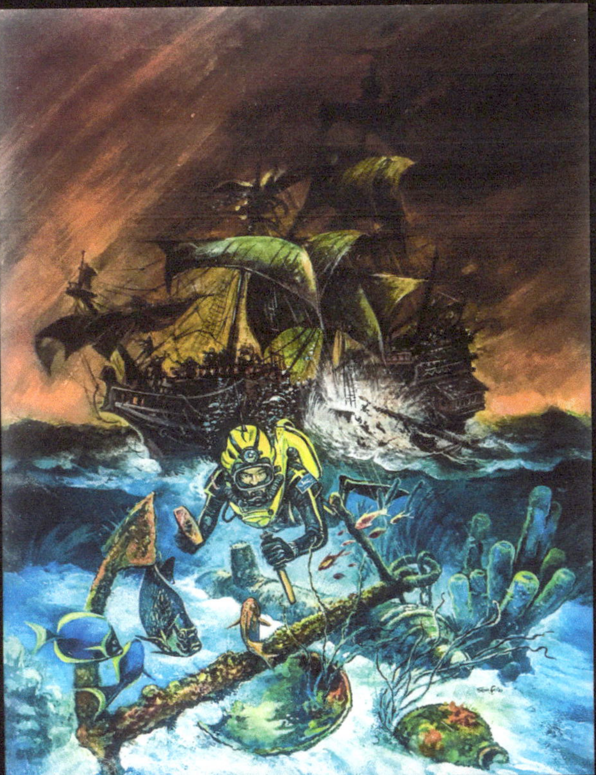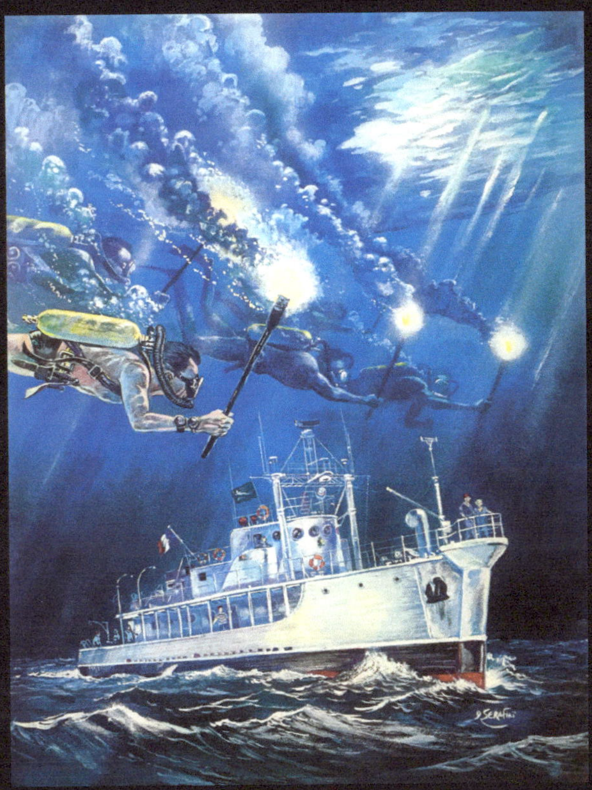

The underwater world is a fascinating and mysterious universe. Cousteau made over 150 films on diverse topics that were an endless source of inspiration for my books. There were limitless subjects for the covers of my Cousteau book series... sharks, the history of sunken treasures... and of course, the Calypso team itself.

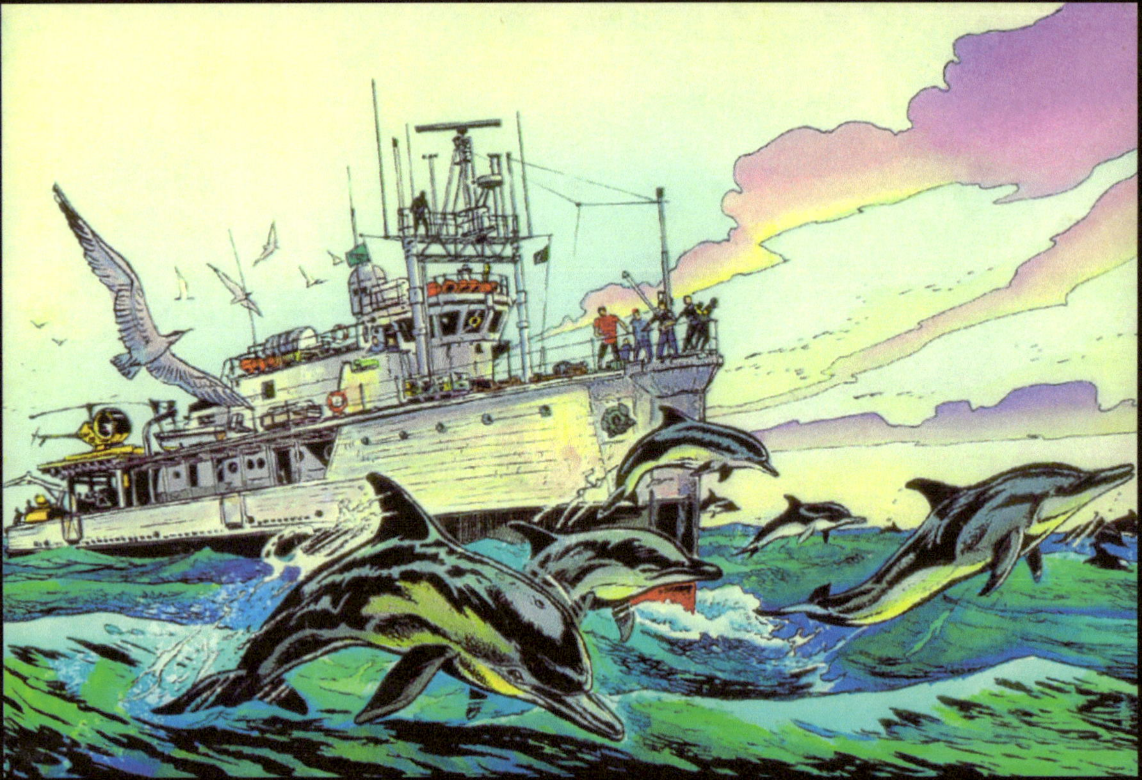

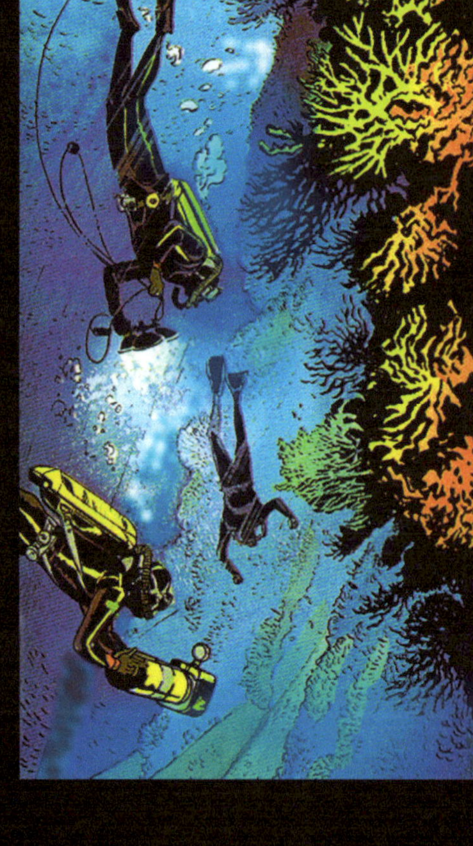

The Calypso, the legendary oceanographic boat accompanied by a pod of dolphins.
The Calypso was the symbol of scientific underwater exploration for over 50 years.

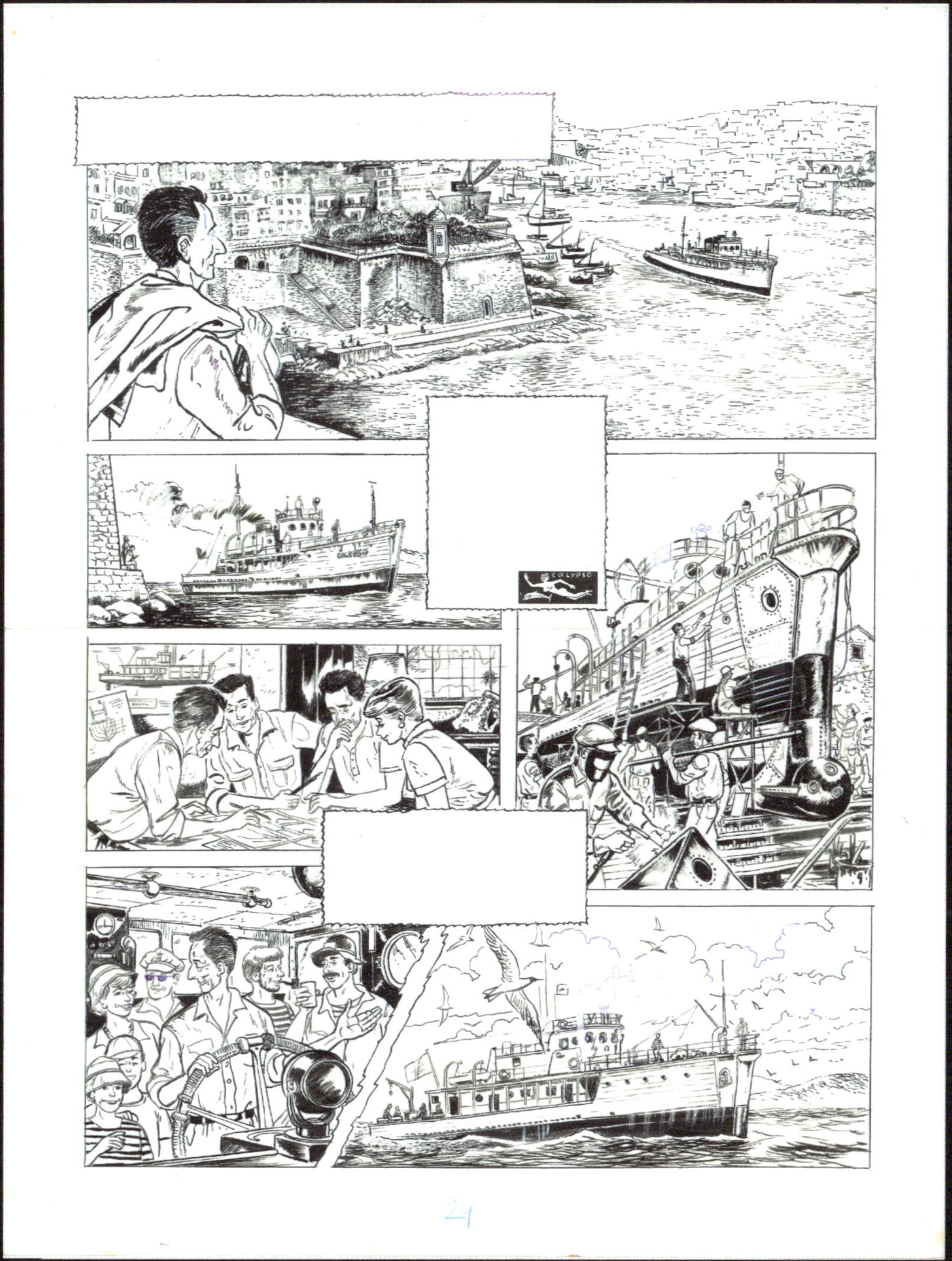

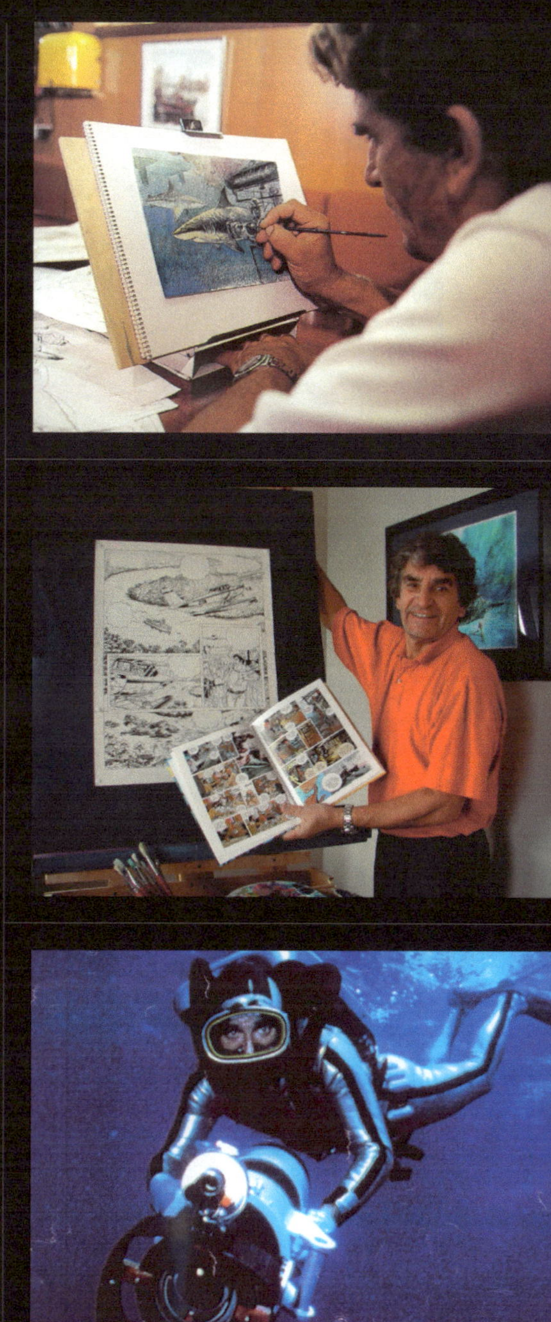

From the sketches I made during the Cousteau expeditions, I created the original drawings for my children's' book series. The drawings were done with pen and brush, using Indian ink and watercolors.

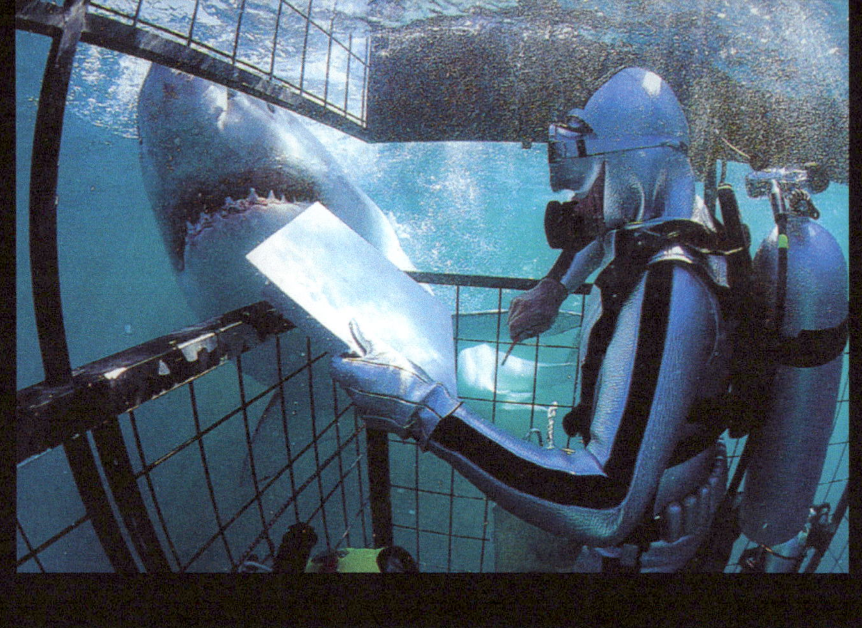

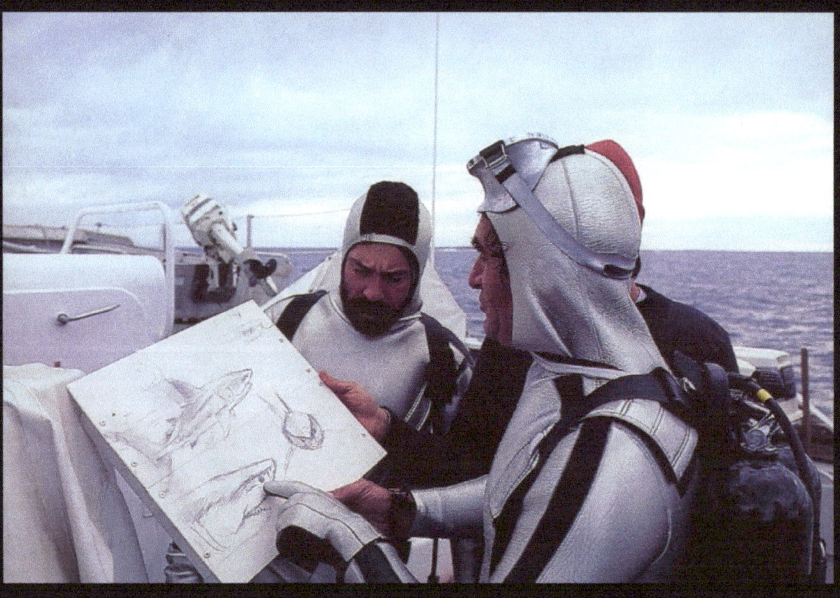

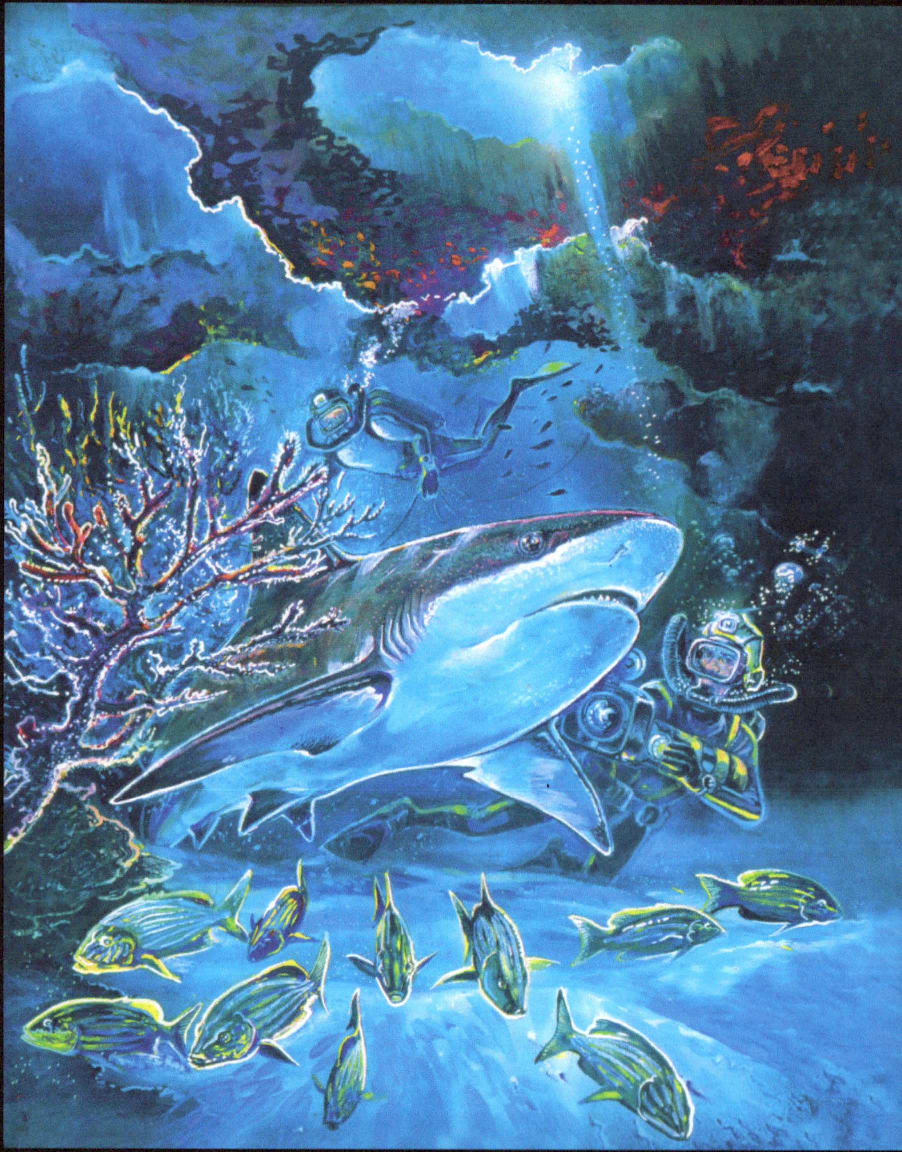

Diving and sketching the great-white shark in the shark cage.
Back on board of the Alcyone, I discussed my drawings with the
team, reworked my sketches and put them in color.

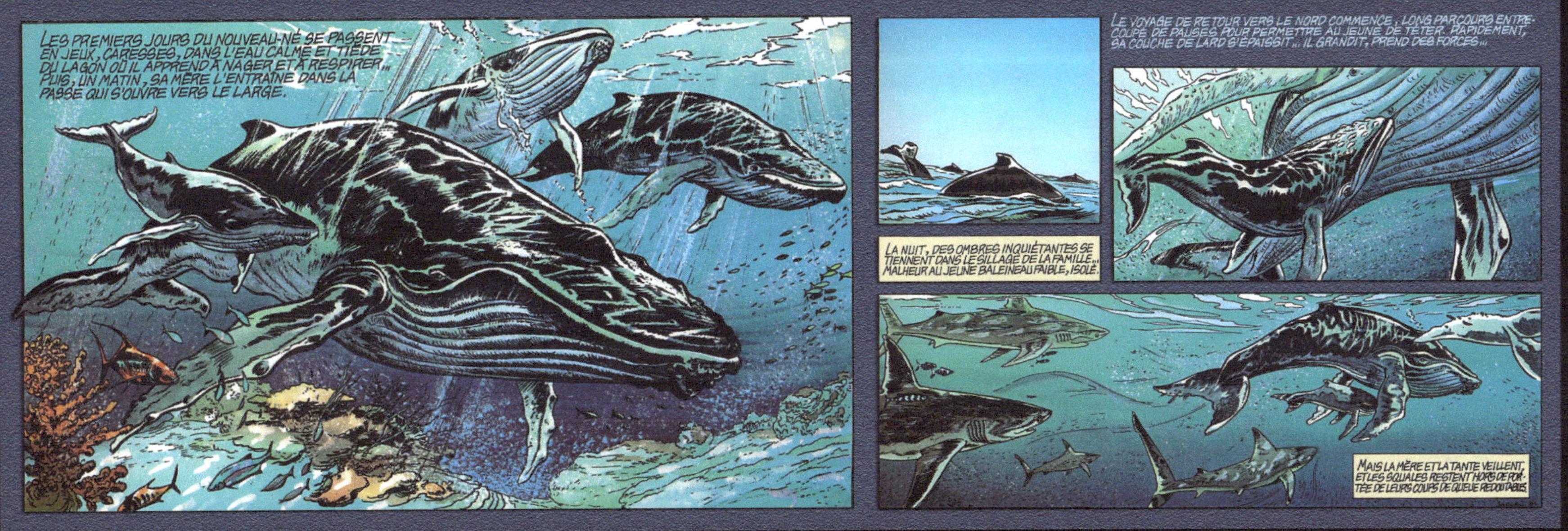

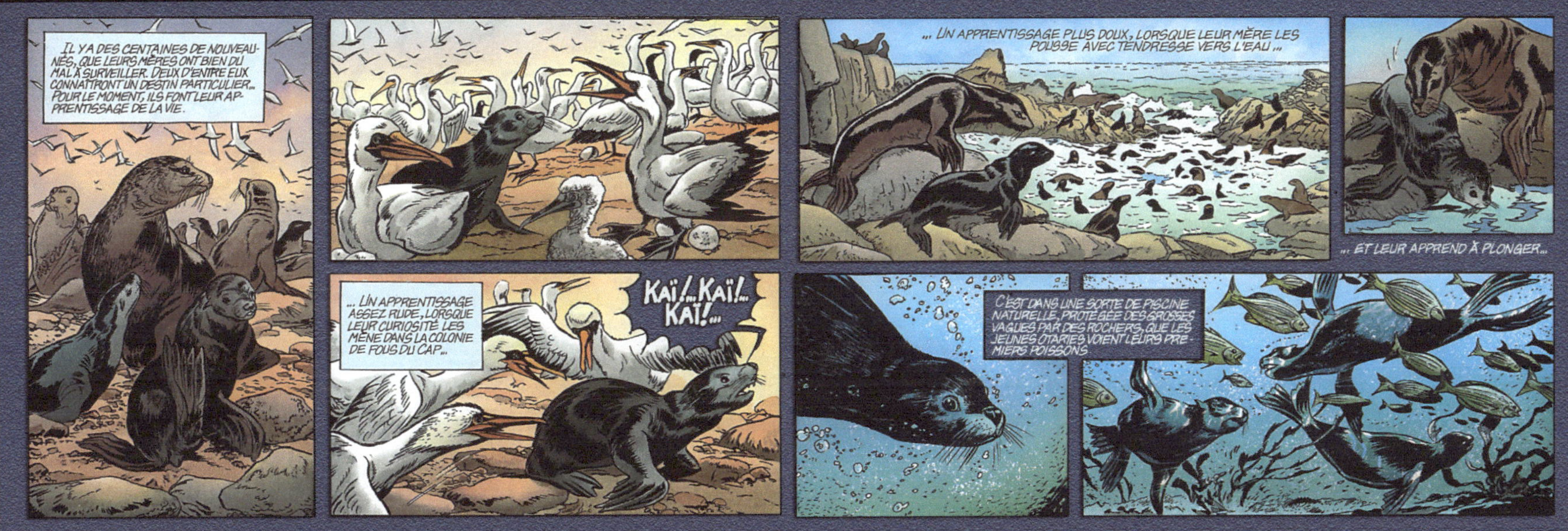

Each album has 46 original drawings. With 17 different albums plus the cover paintings, I made more than 1000 drawings. It was a big job, which took me 20 years to complete and I loved every minute of it. After the death of Jacques-Yves Cousteau things grinded to a halt and I returned to the sea.

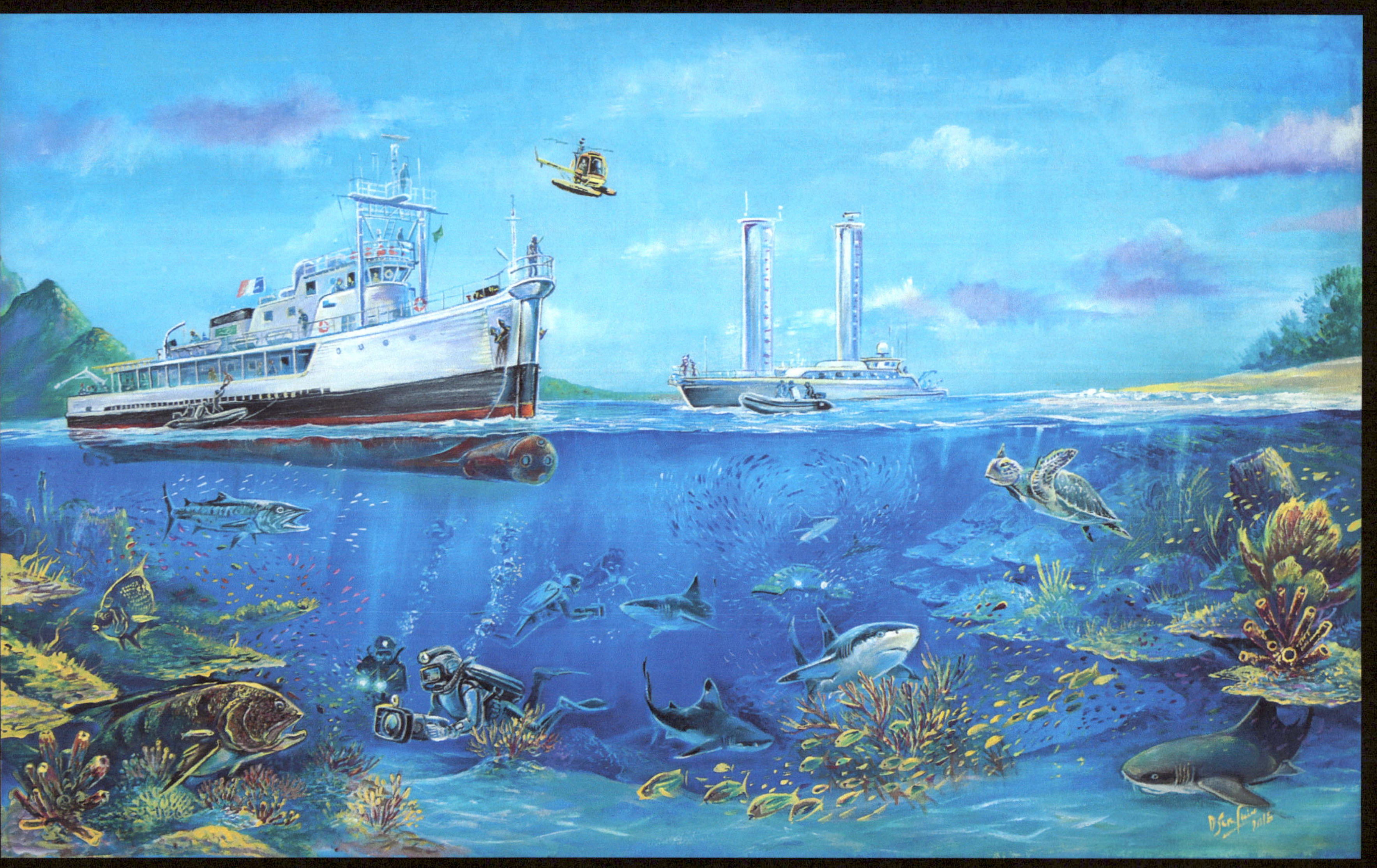

I have fantastic memories of my time on the Calypso and Alcyone. In my paintings, I try to share this sense of happiness I had, working as part of the team. The complexity of the Cousteau expeditions as well as the team effort required is expressed in this painting.

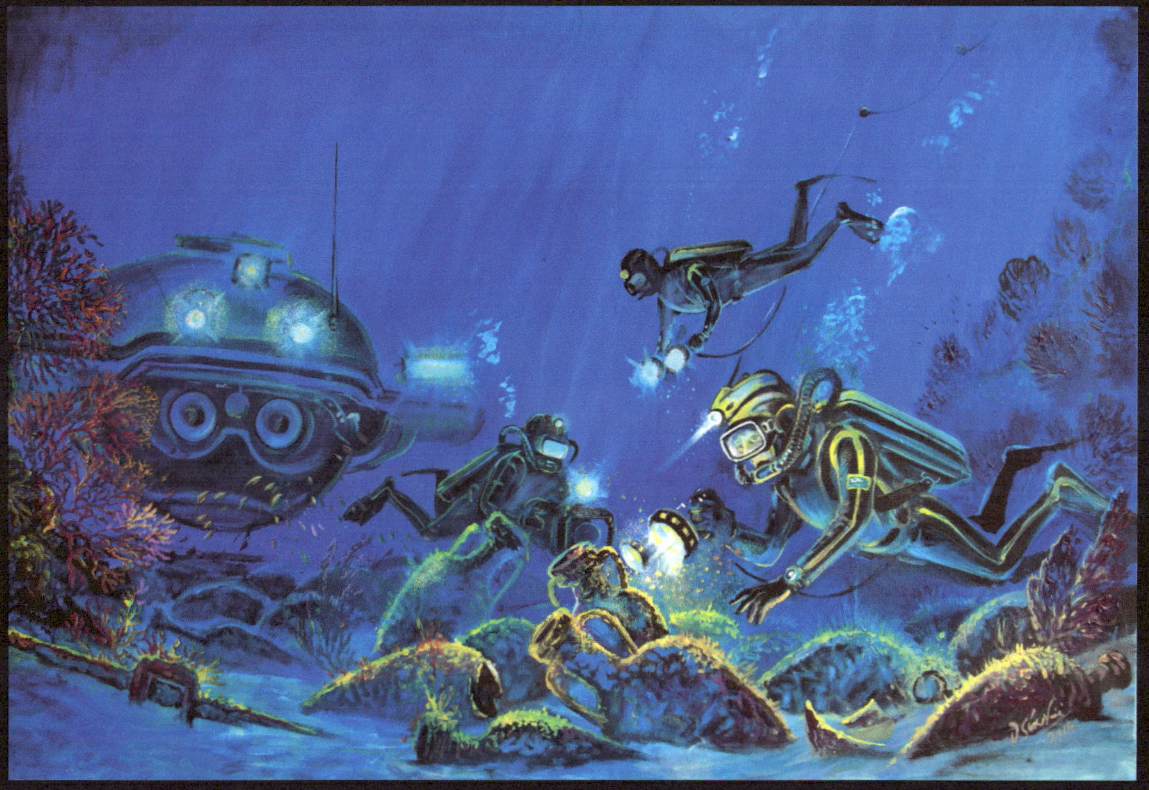

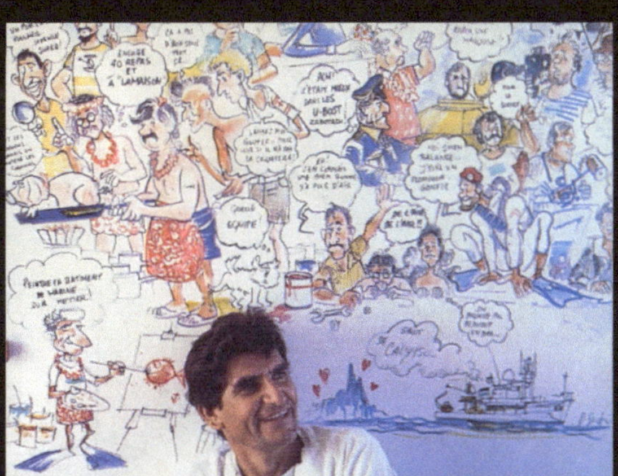

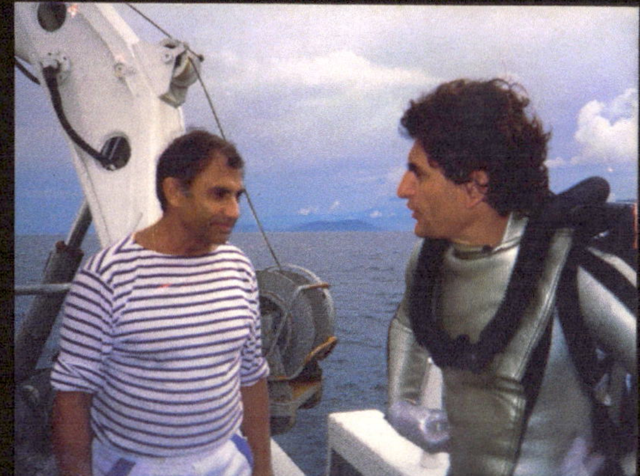

Jacques-Yves Cousteau, Simone Cousteau and Falco are still very much alive in my memory.
Each breath I take underwater is like a breath from these old friends from the Cousteau team.

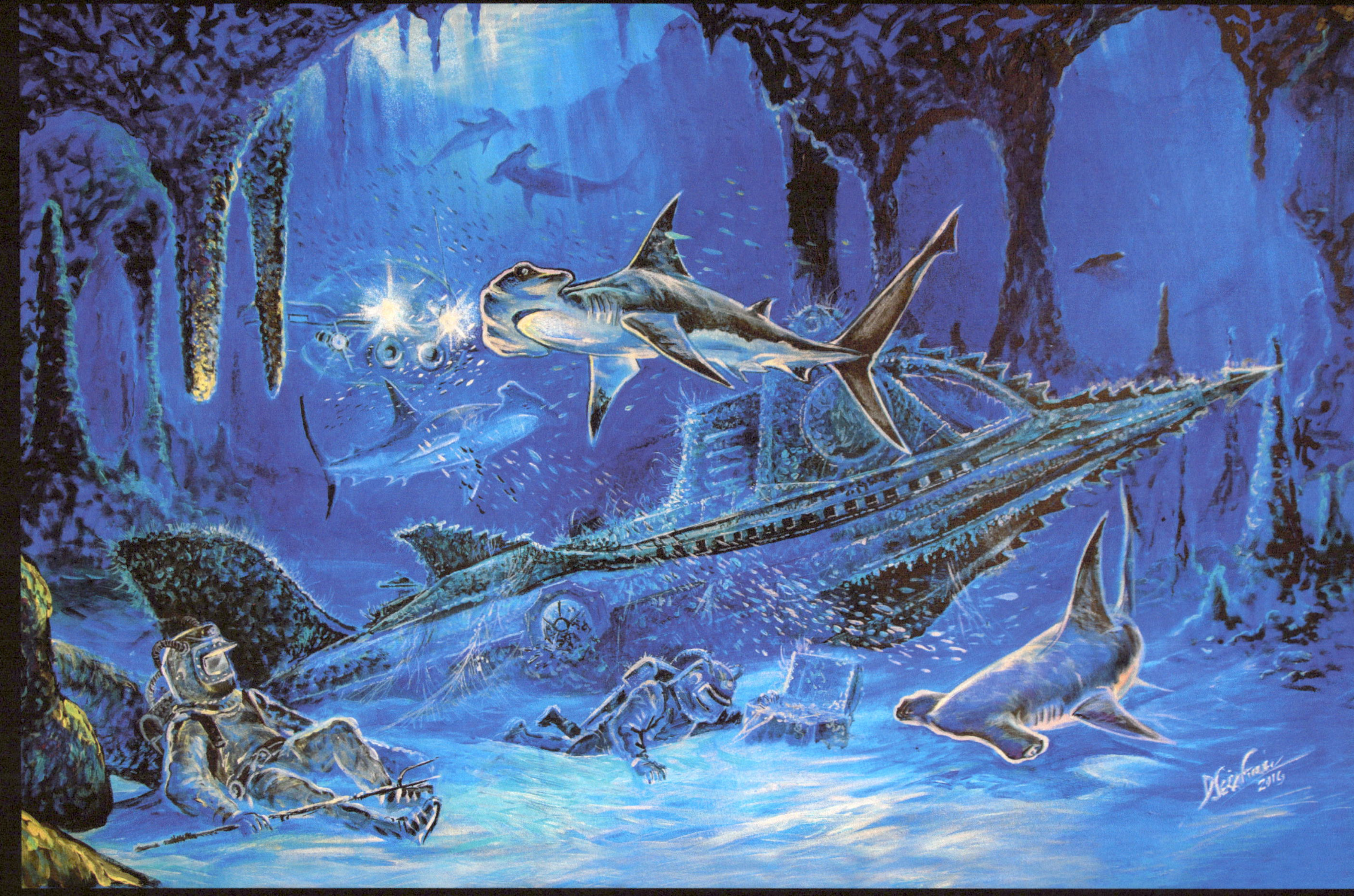

Captain Nemo with his submarine Nautilus, featured in «20 000 Leagues Under the Sea» made thousands of readers and cinephiles dream. But Cousteau actually lived the dreams of Jules Verne. In this painting, I imagined Cousteau, on board his underwater diving saucer, discovering the wreck of Nautilus, sunk inside an underwater cave.

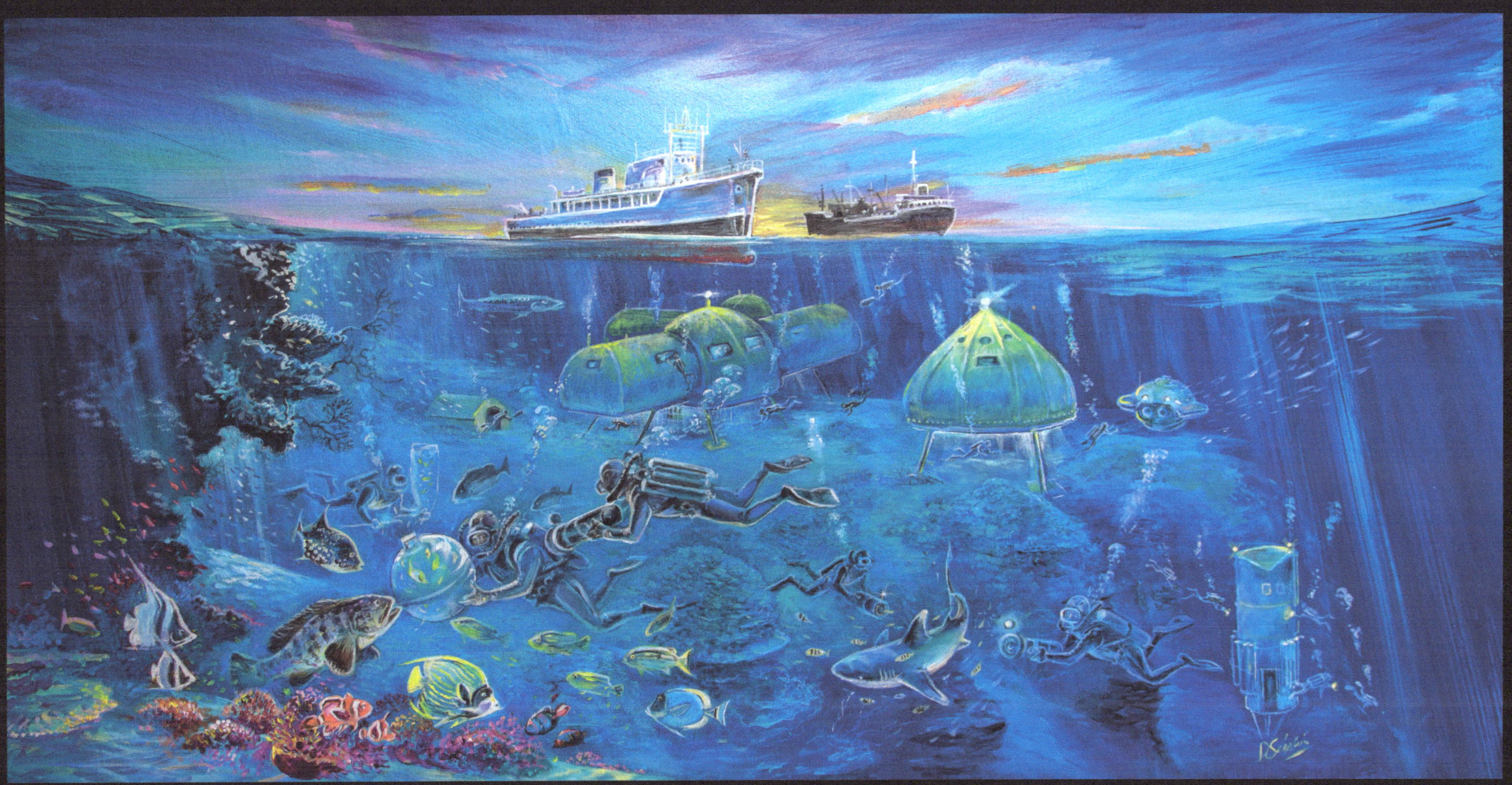

In the 1970s, Cousteau and his team organized a series of expeditions to colonize the shallow coastal waters under the sea. In these underwater structures, the aquanauts lived and worked in saturation and did not have to come to the surface. It was a beautiful and ambitious dream. I also dreamed of one day when I could live and paint in my underwater painting studio. This painting is of Precontinent 2, the underwater village that Cousteau built in the Red Sea in Sudan. While living in Precontinent 2, the Cousteau divers carried out various experiments. The work appears in the book «Mer Rouge Eau Bleue».

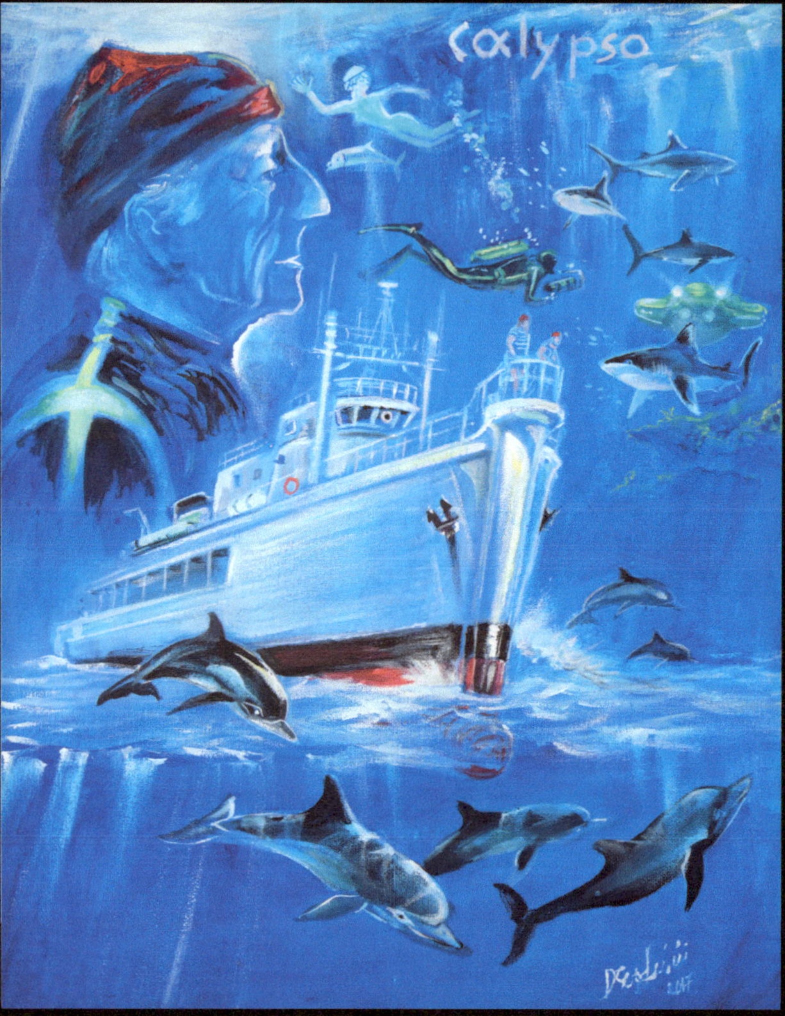
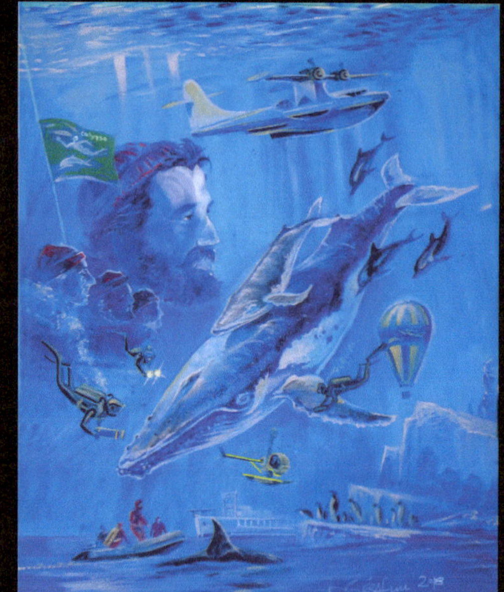
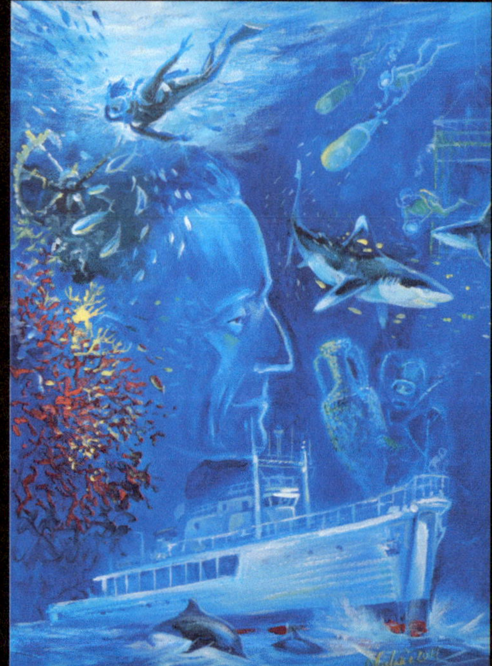
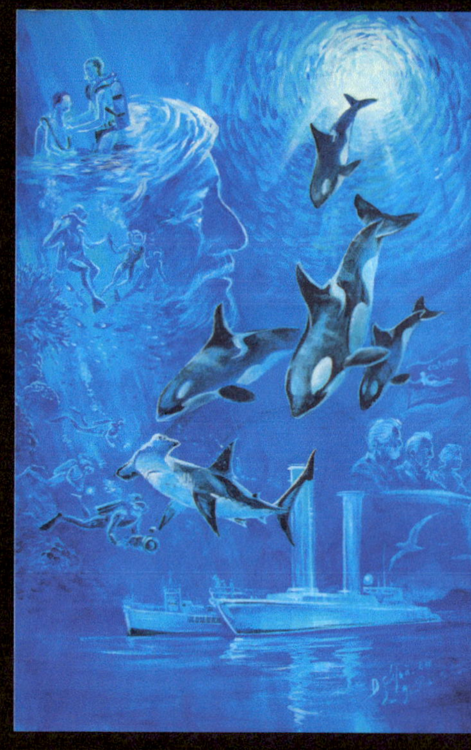
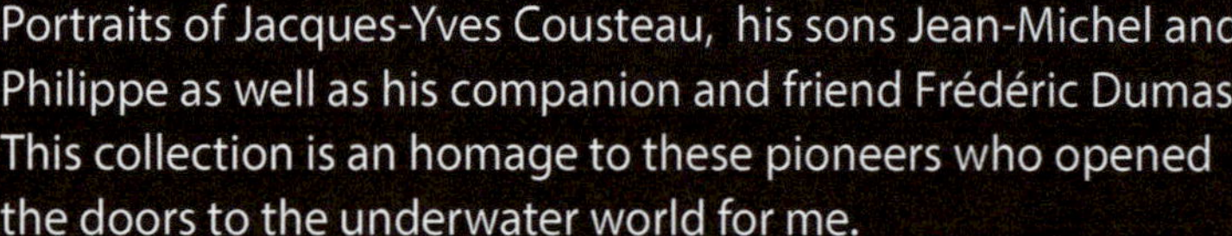

Portraits of Jacques-Yves Cousteau, his sons Jean-Michel and Philippe as well as his companion and friend Frédéric Dumas. This collection is an homage to these pioneers who opened the doors to the underwater world for me.

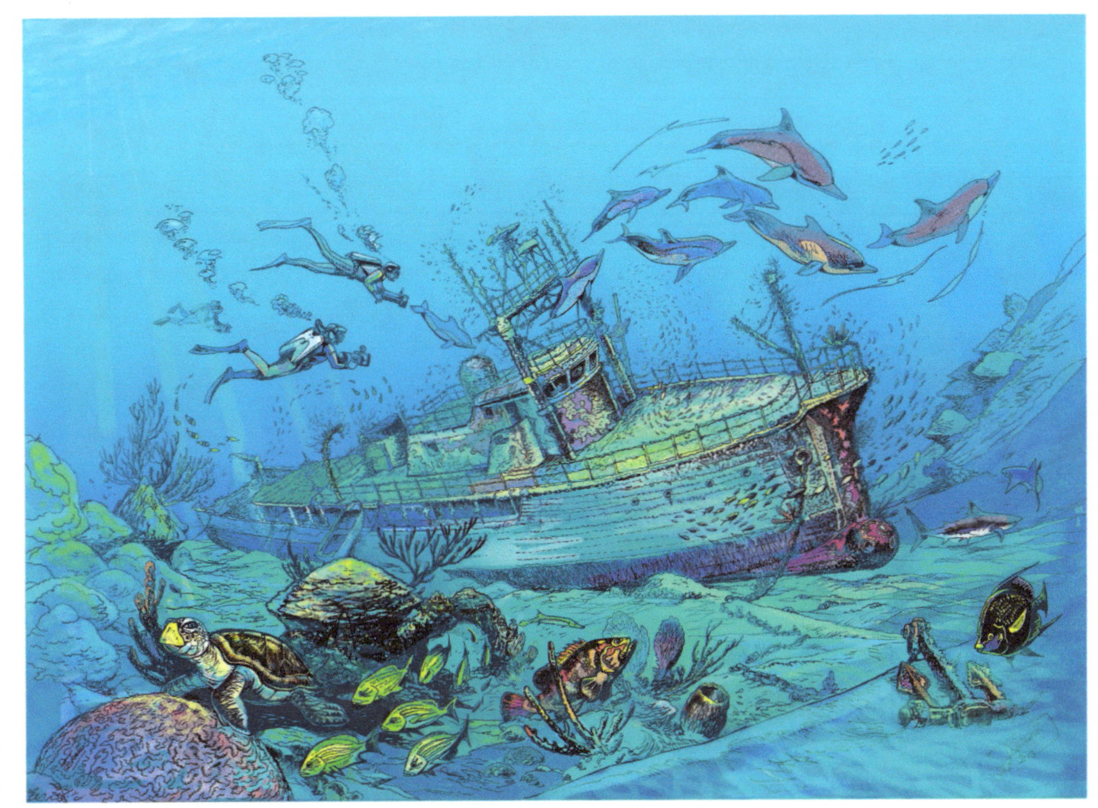

CALYPSO'S FINAL JOURNEY

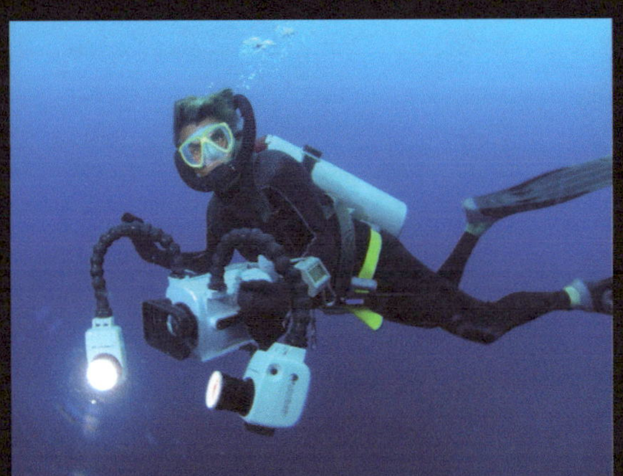

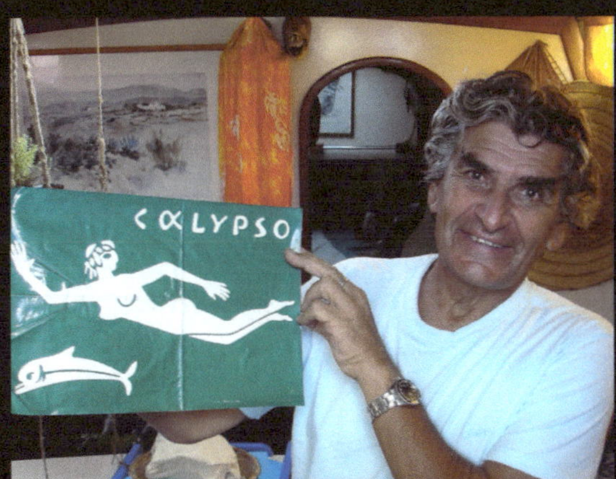

Cousteau hoped that the Calypso would finish its life under the sea. Unfortunately, Calypso sunk in the Singapore harbor. The spirit of the Calypso is still alive and well on board my sailboat.

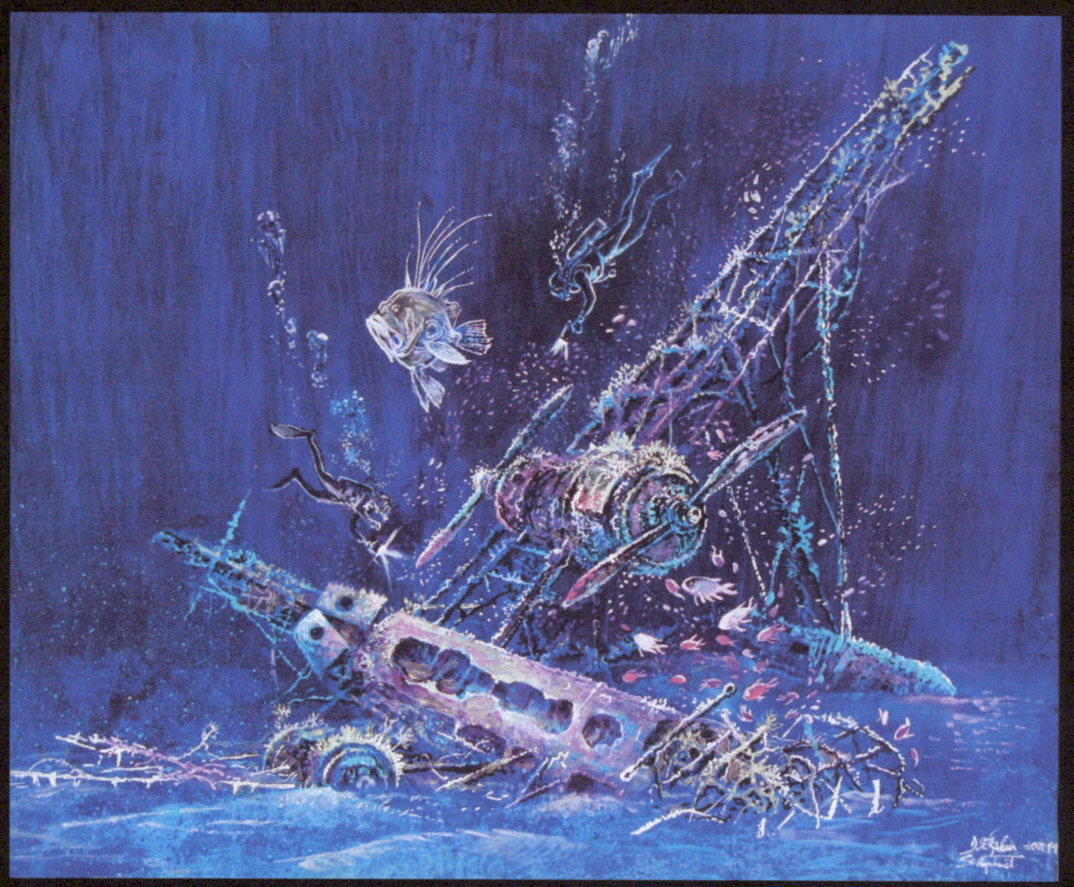

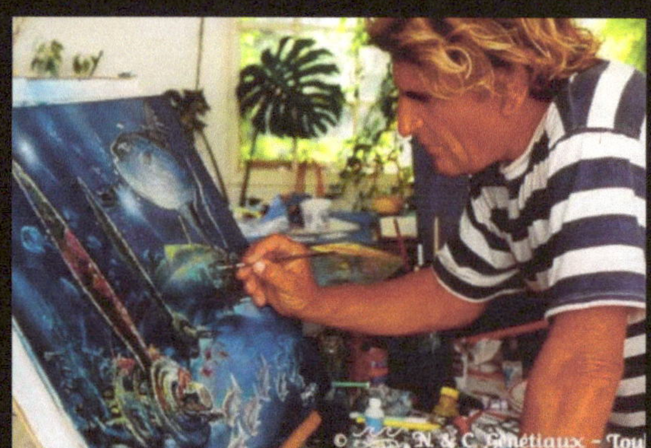

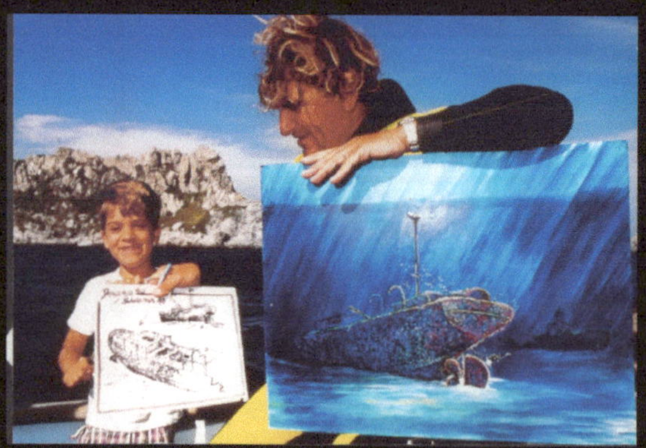

My passion for shipwrecks led me to the Mediterranean, the Red Sea and the Caribbean.
My children Enzo, Cécile and Laure joined me from time to time on my adventures.

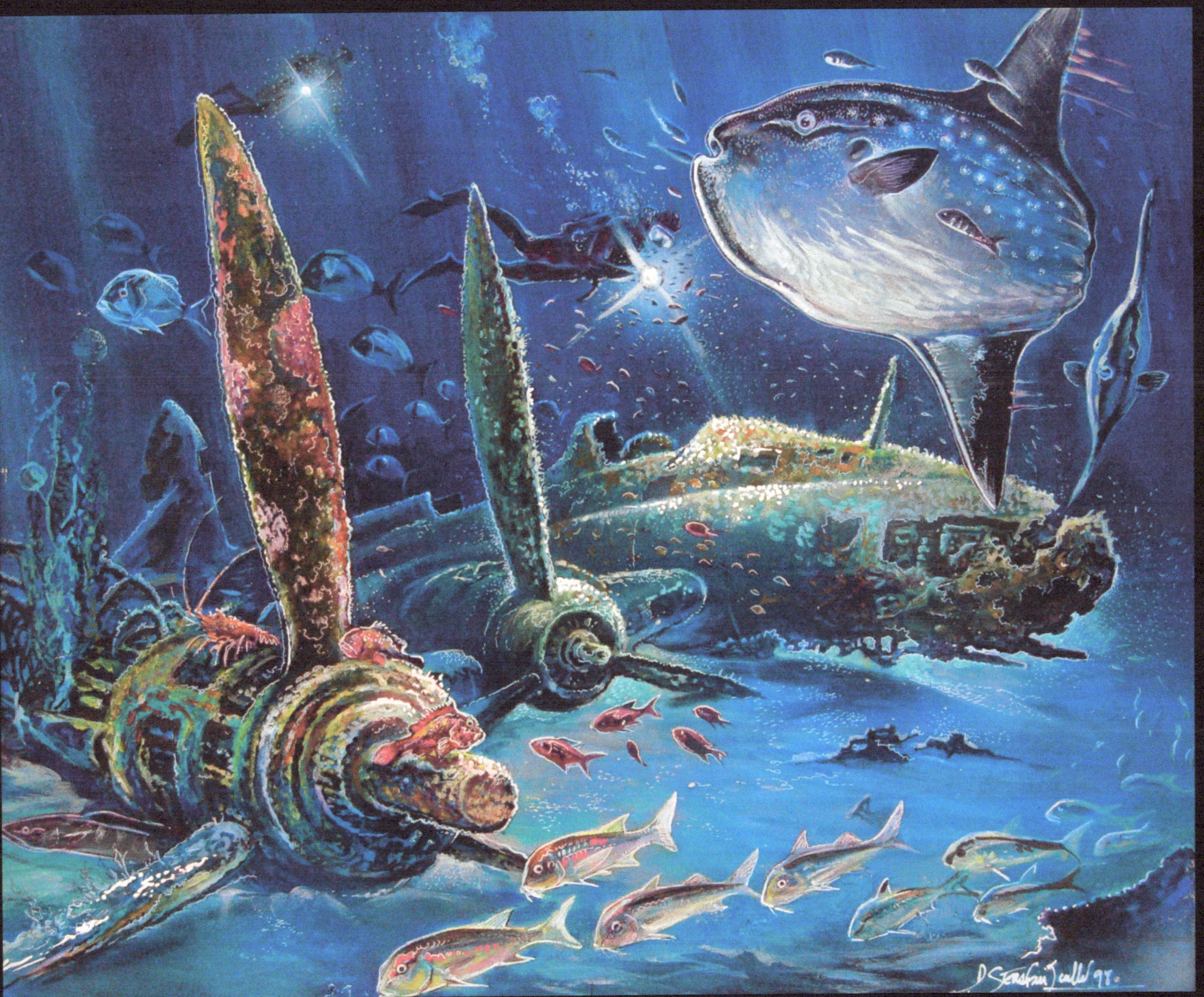

This Lightning P38 airplane sunk in 135 feet of water in the bay of la Ciotat in France. Saint Exupéry, author of "The Little Prince," was flying the same type of fighter plane when he disappeared. The wreck site is a meeting place for sunfish.

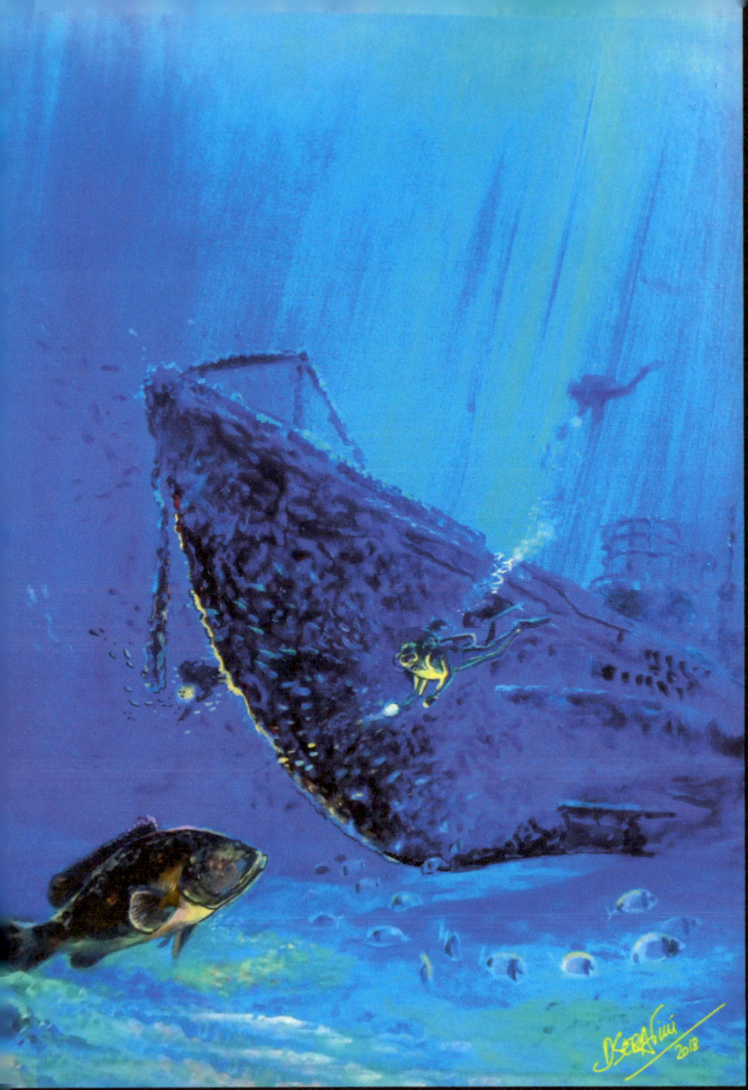

Together with my friends, I dove on these iconic shipwrecks in the Mediterranean. The Rubis, a WW11 submarine is in 150 feet of water. And this old tugboat lies in front of the Oceanographic Museum of Monaco. So many stunning subjects for a series of wreck paintings.

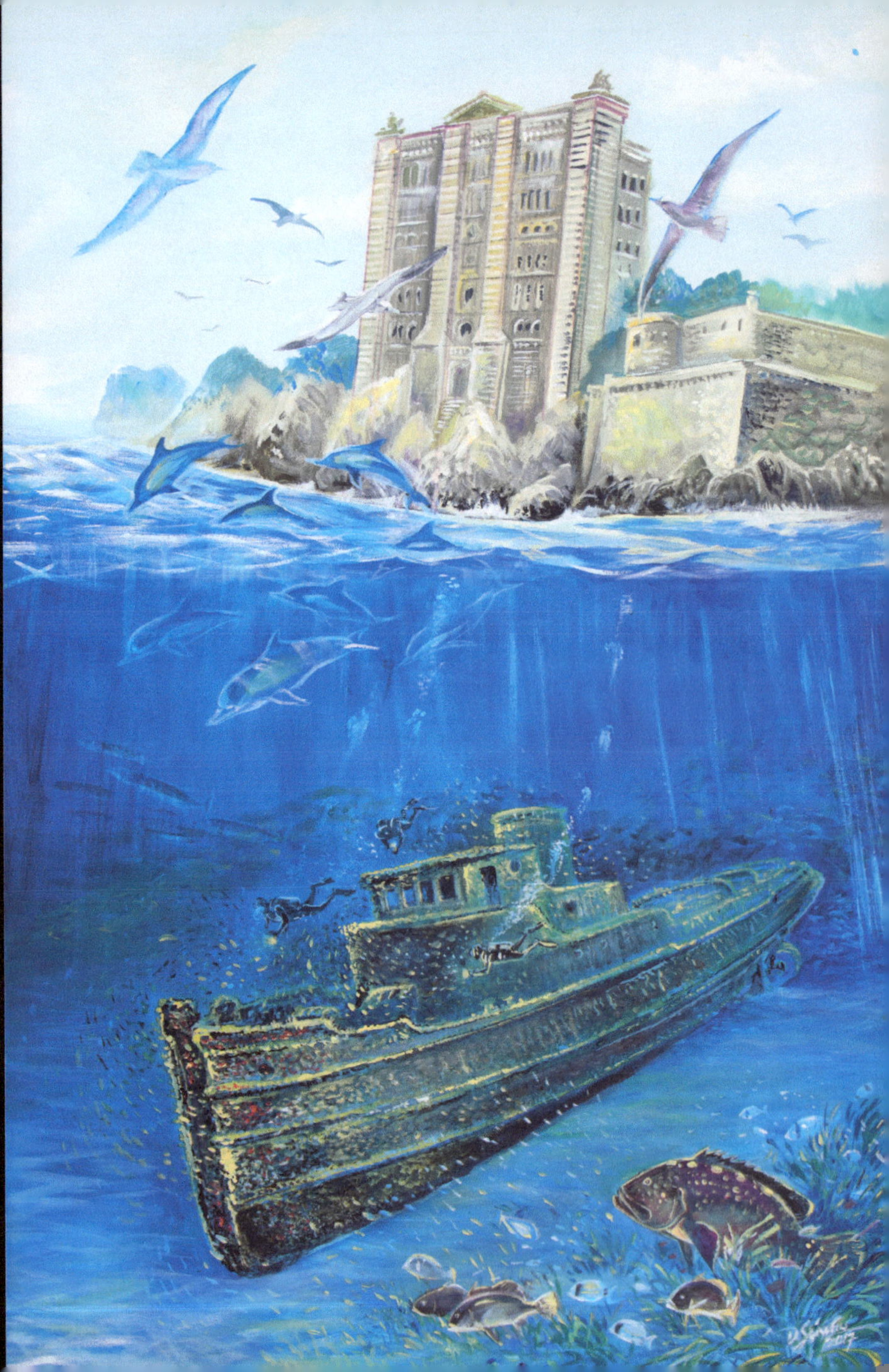

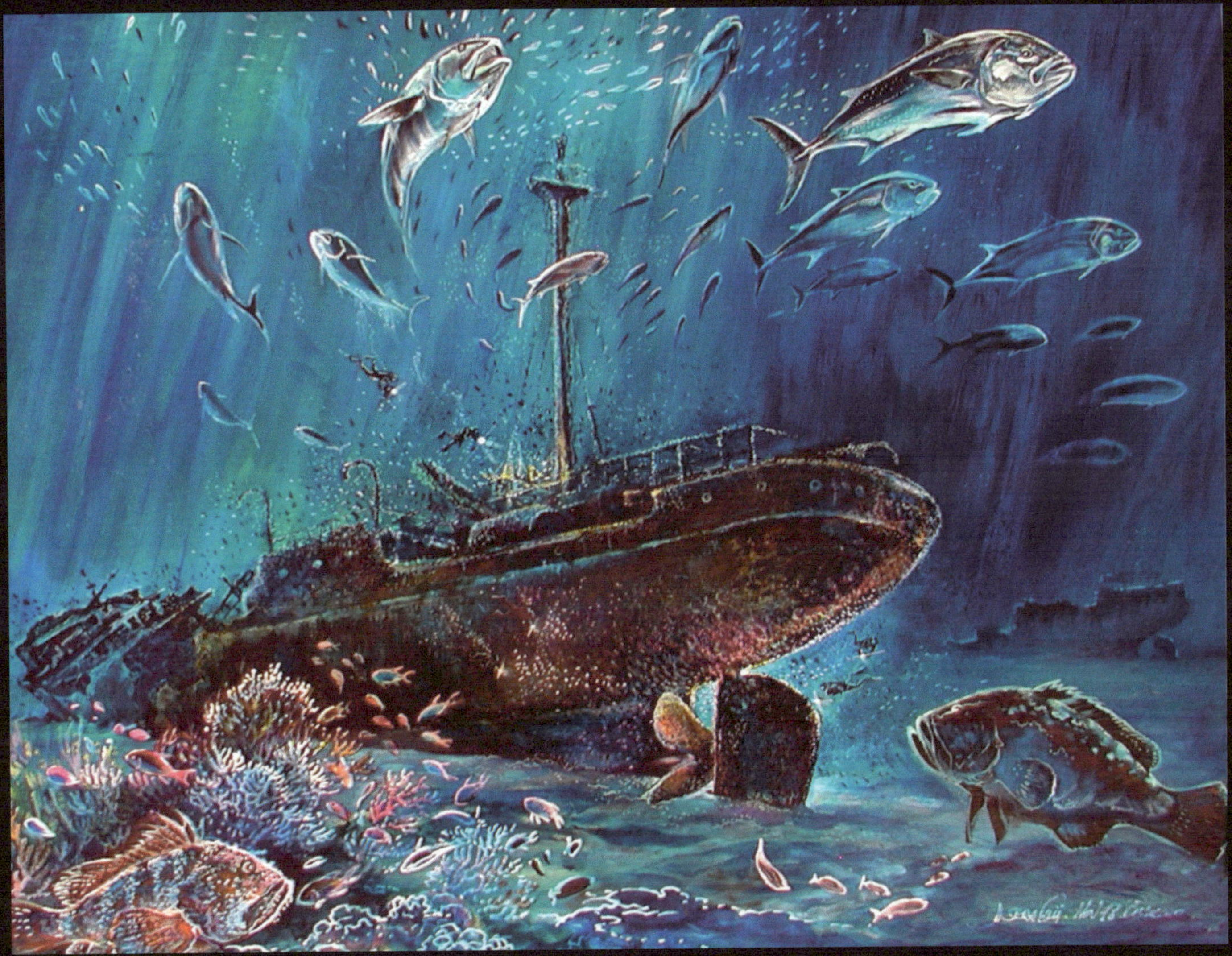

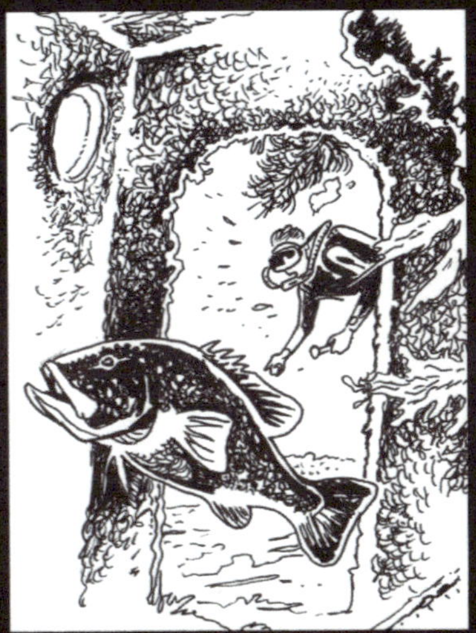

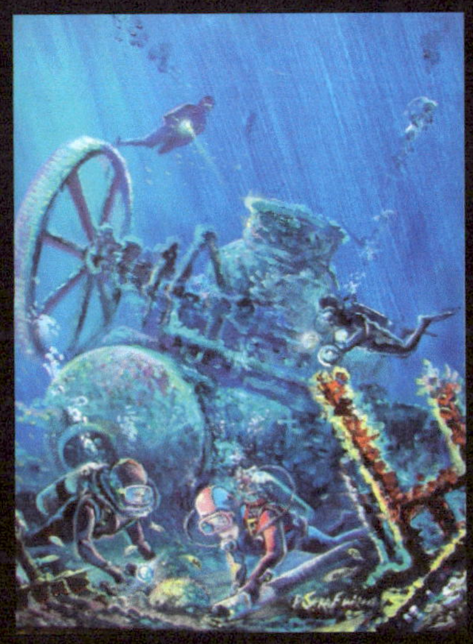

Some shipwrecks like the Donator have become legendary dive sites. This freighter hit a German mine between the island of Porquerolles and Port Cros in the south of France and is now sitting at 165 feet of water. Covered with red gorgonians, the wreck is a meeting place for groupers, snappers and jacks.

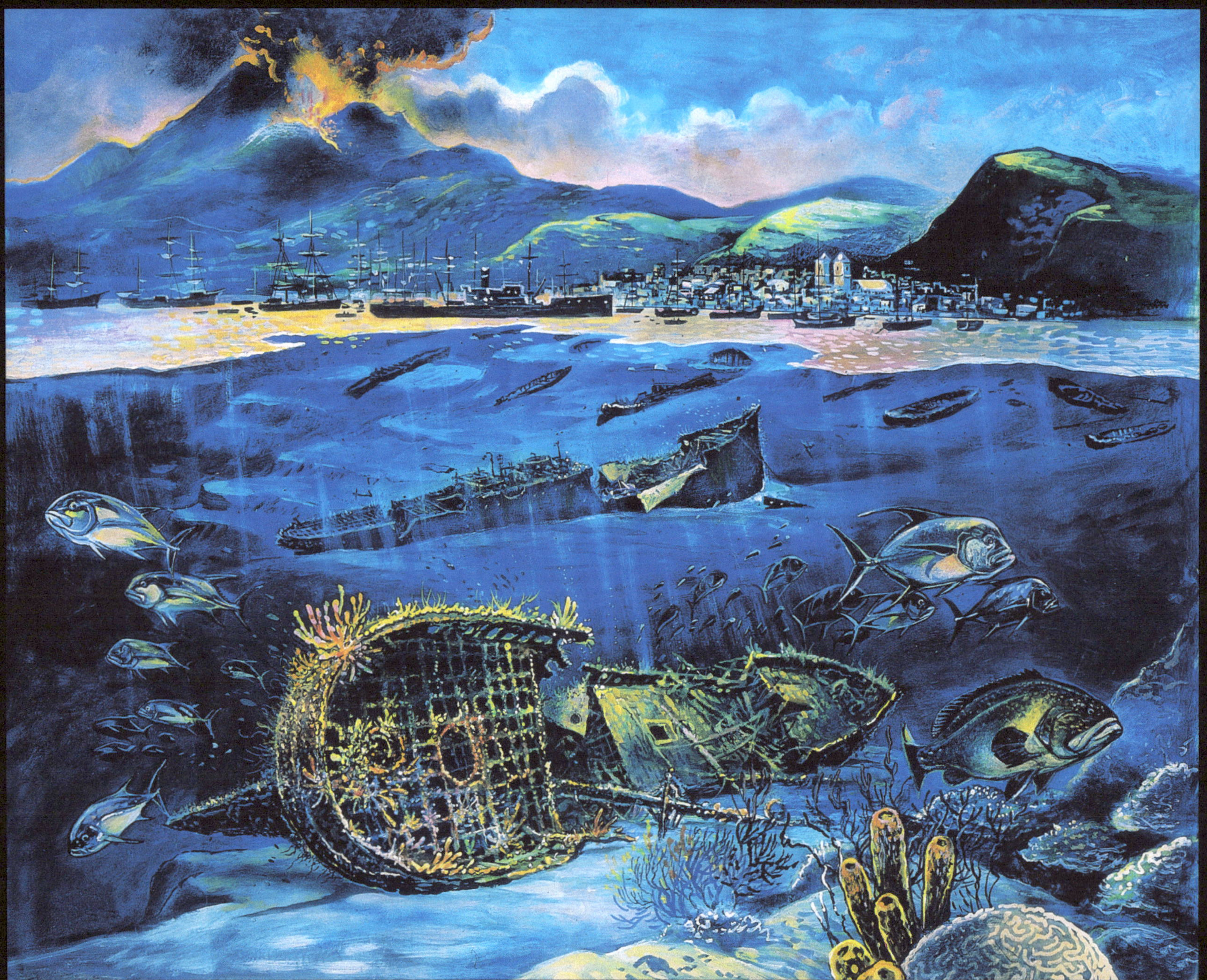

The bay of Saint-Pierre in Martinique. On May 8, 1902, mount Pelée erupted and rained a storm of fire on the city, destroying everything in its path and killing over 30,000 people. More than 15 boats sunk.

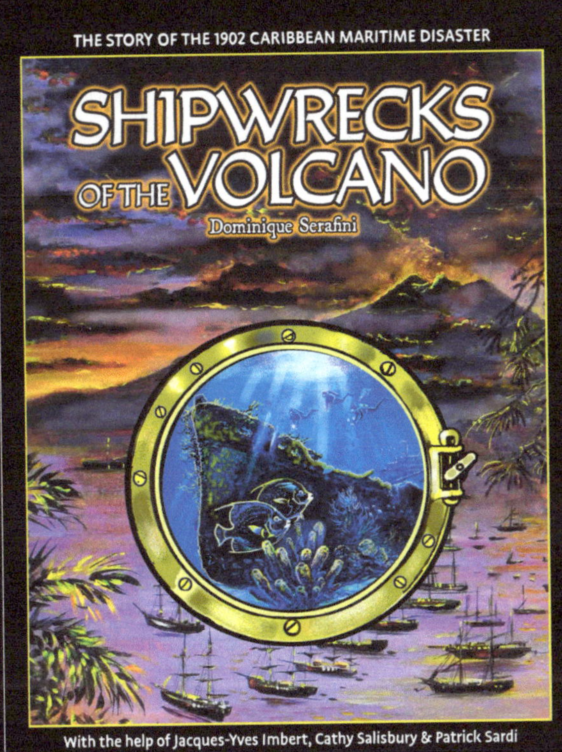

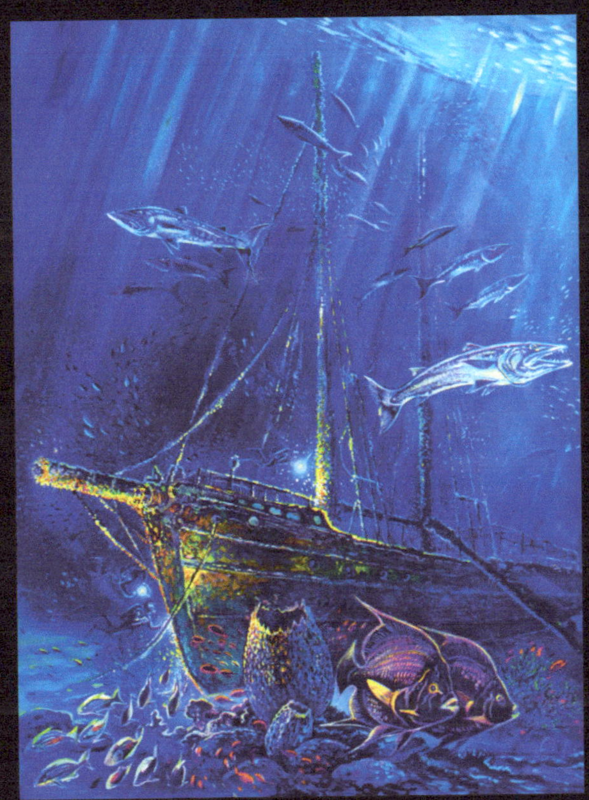

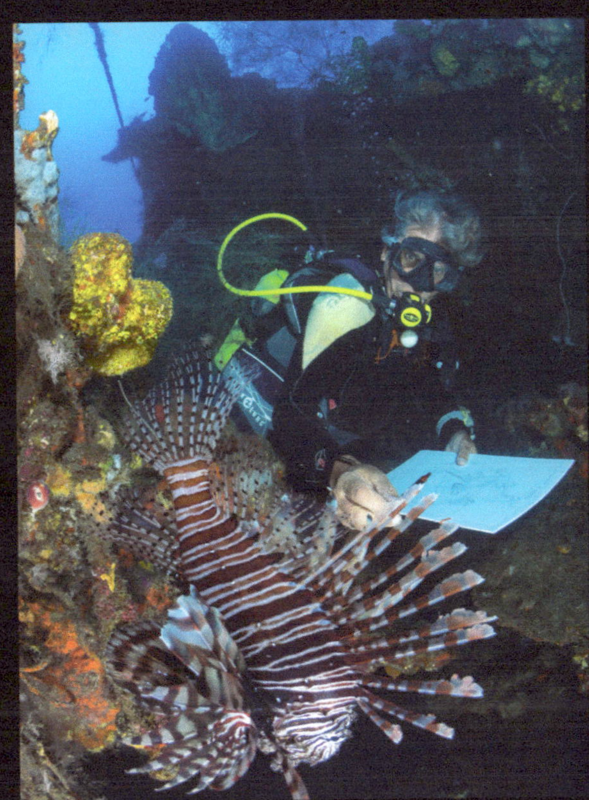

In my graphic novel that I created in 2015 called «Shipwrecks of the Volcano», I tell the story of the boats that sunk in the bay of Saint-Pierre in 1902. Now well populated by lionfish, The Nahoon was sunk in 100 feet of water to make an artificial reef near Fort-de-France, Martinique.

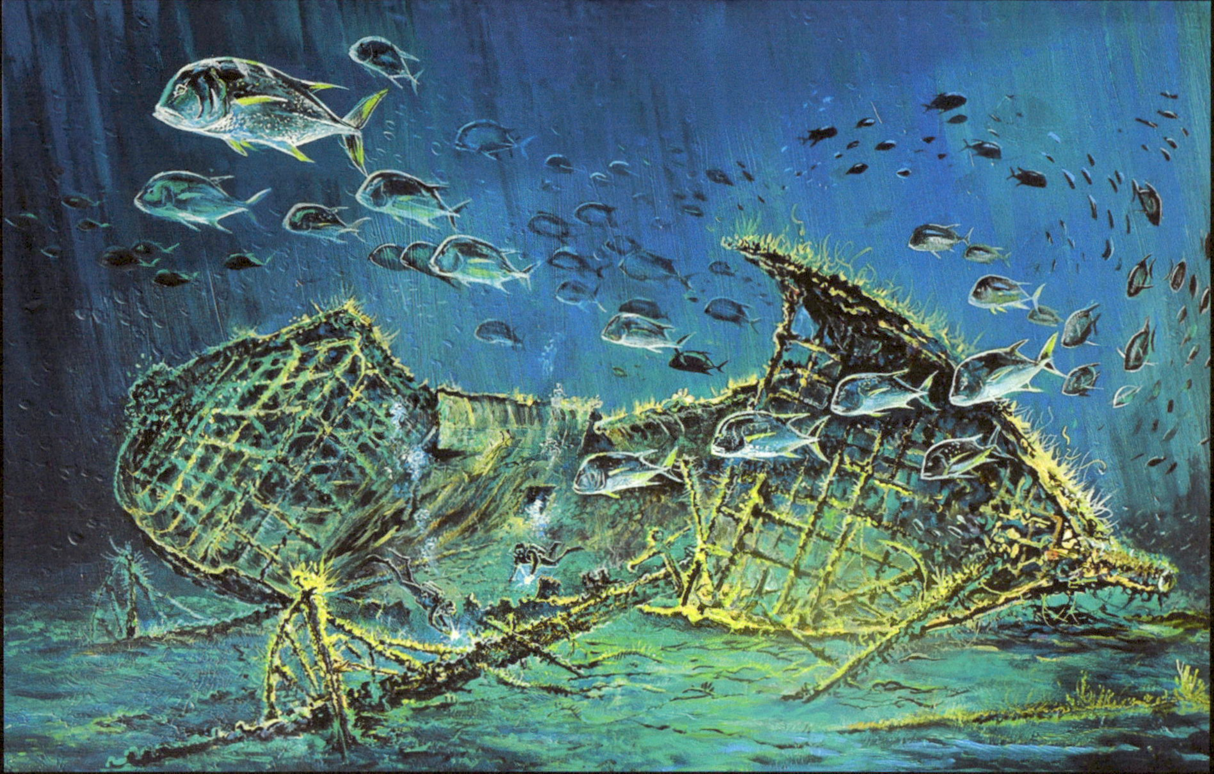

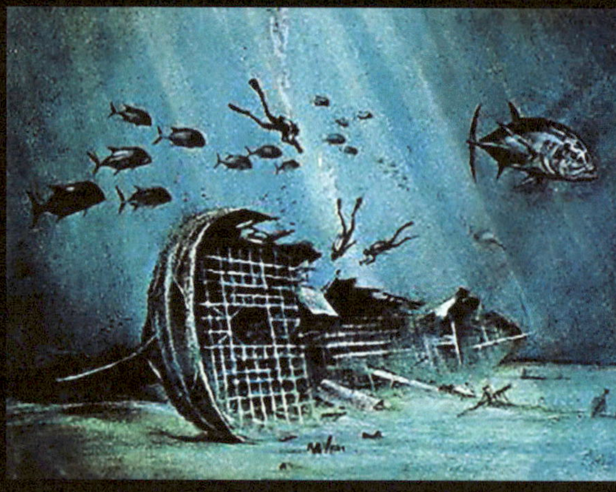

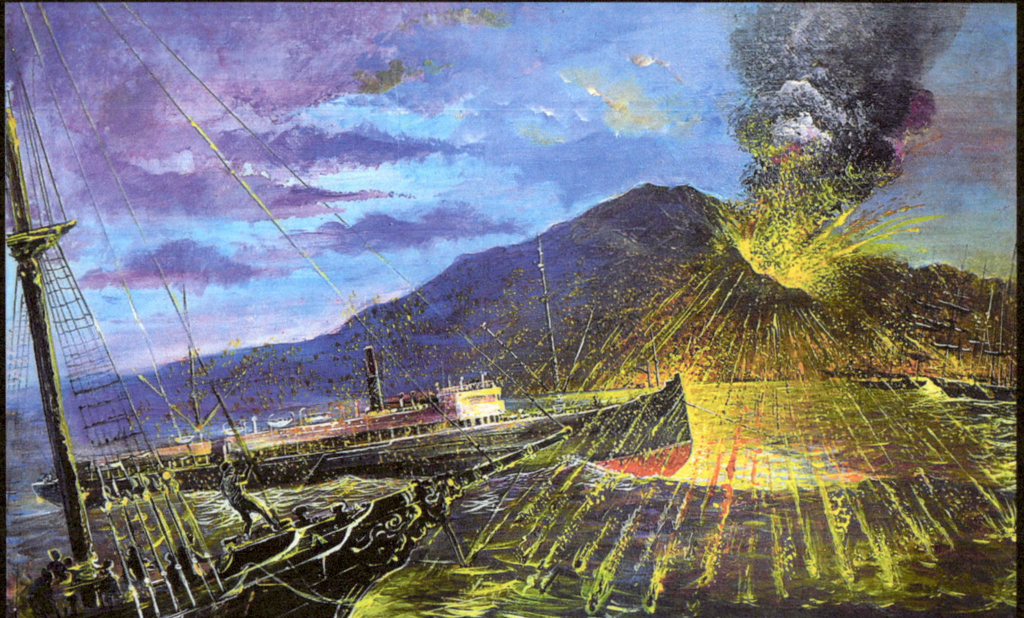

The dream of many scuba divers is to find an unknown shipwreck. I had that privilege one day in 1983 when I found and explored this virgin three-mast clipper at a depth of 280 feet. I created a sketch on my first dive. The Tamaya lay on the edge of an underwater abyss. Its existence had eluded researchers, including Cousteau, who had searched for it in the bay of Saint-Pierre.

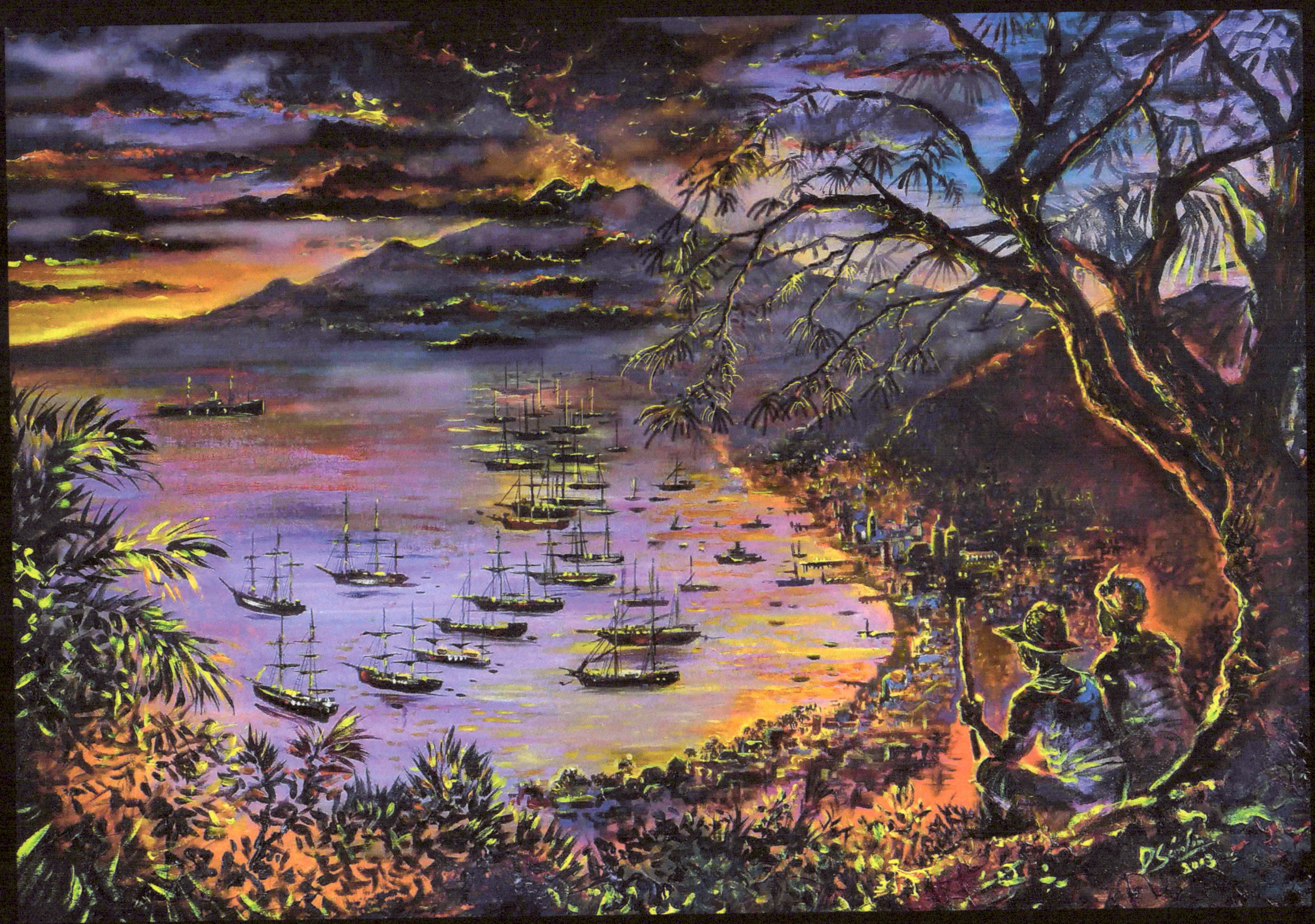

The night before the eruption of 1902 in Saint-Pierre. A couple sit under a tree and watch the red flames of Mount Pelée, lighting up the evening sky.

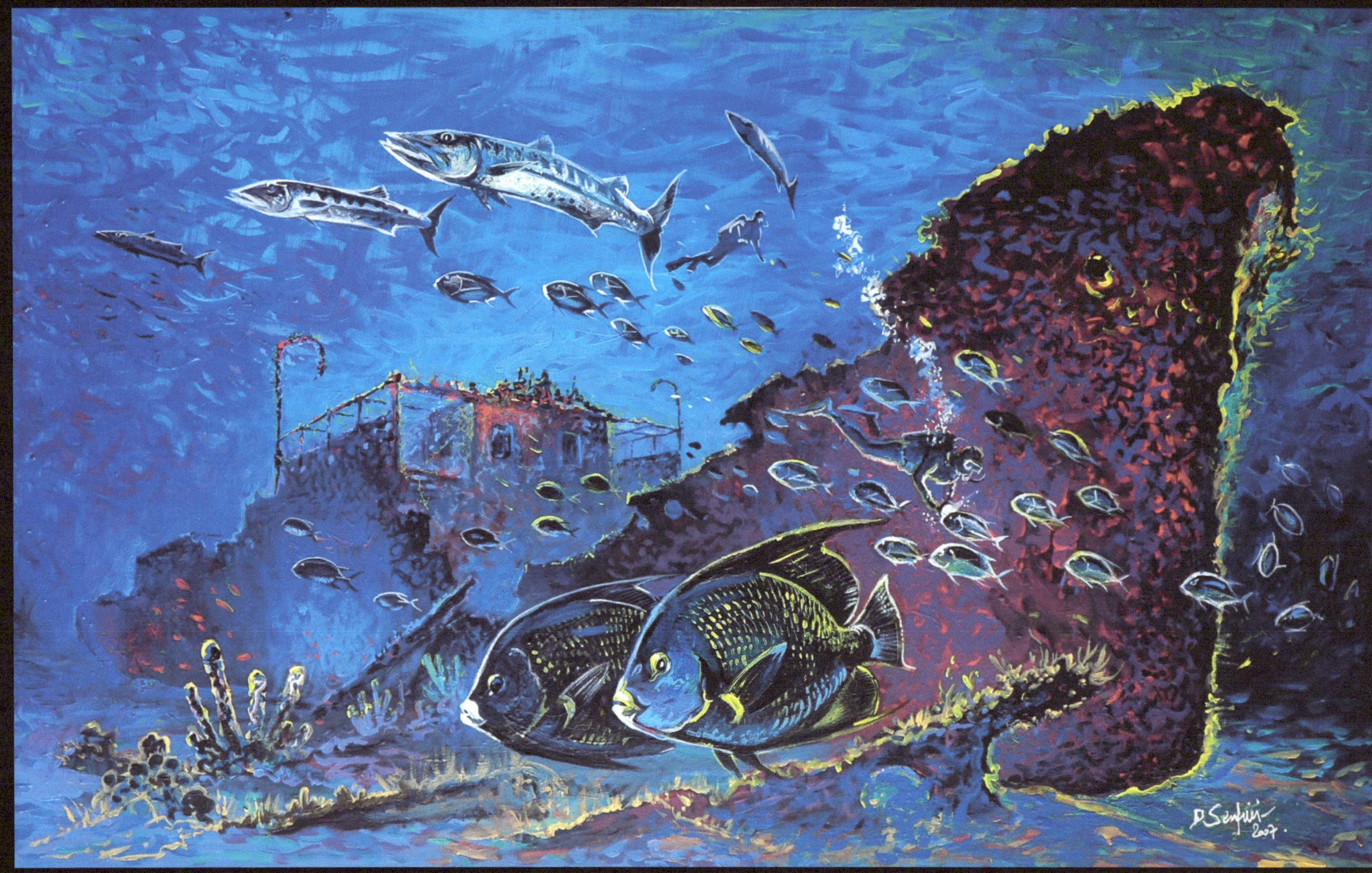

The wreck of the Roraima, a large steamship that sank in the bay of Saint-Pierre, Martinique is an historic dive site. The long passageways and the cargo holds as well as the machine room have inspired many of my paintings.

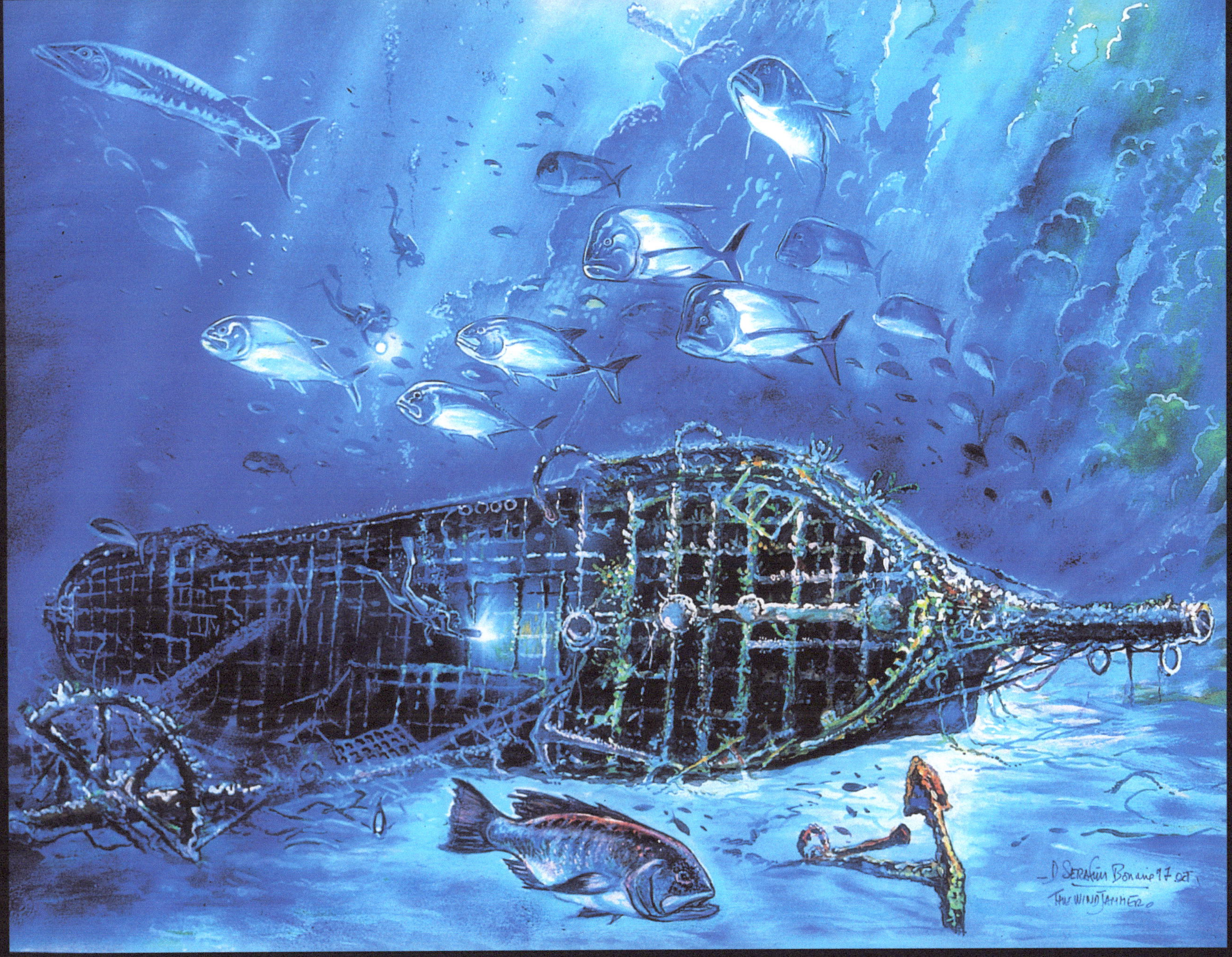

My series of paintings «DreamWrecks» were inspired by the Windjammer shipwreck in Bonaire. I first dove on this three-mast, steel-hulled clipper back in 1997. It was a real phantom wreck, sunk in deep water, 200 feet under the surface.

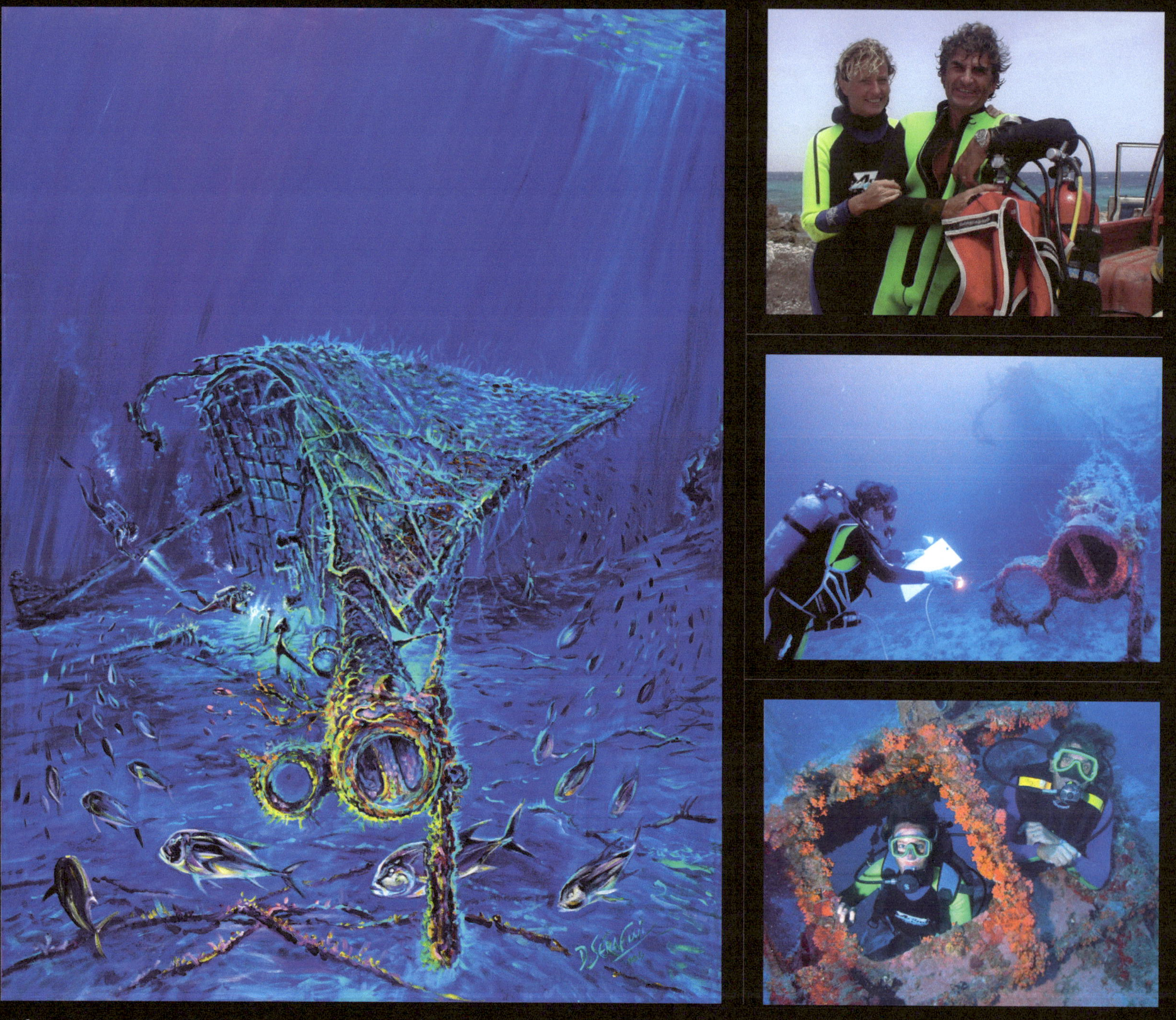

I first explored the Windjammer on my own. I then met Catherine, who like me, was passionate about diving on the wreck. An exceptional diver, Catherine shared many dives with me on the wreck and completed my painterly vision with her underwater photos.

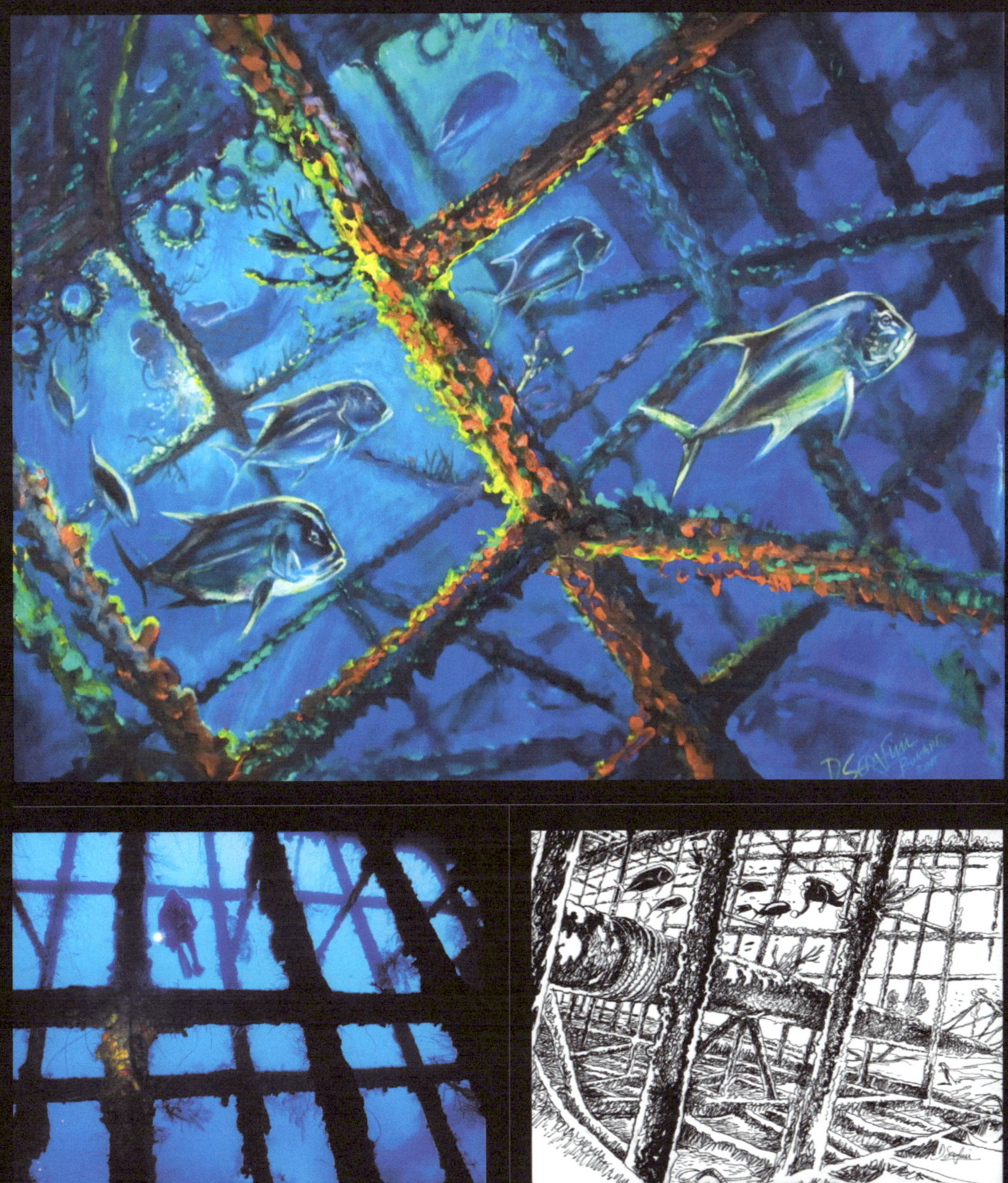

We would penetrate the hull of the old clipper, with great respect, like visiting a sunken cathedral. The sounds of our bubbles resonated throughout the interior.

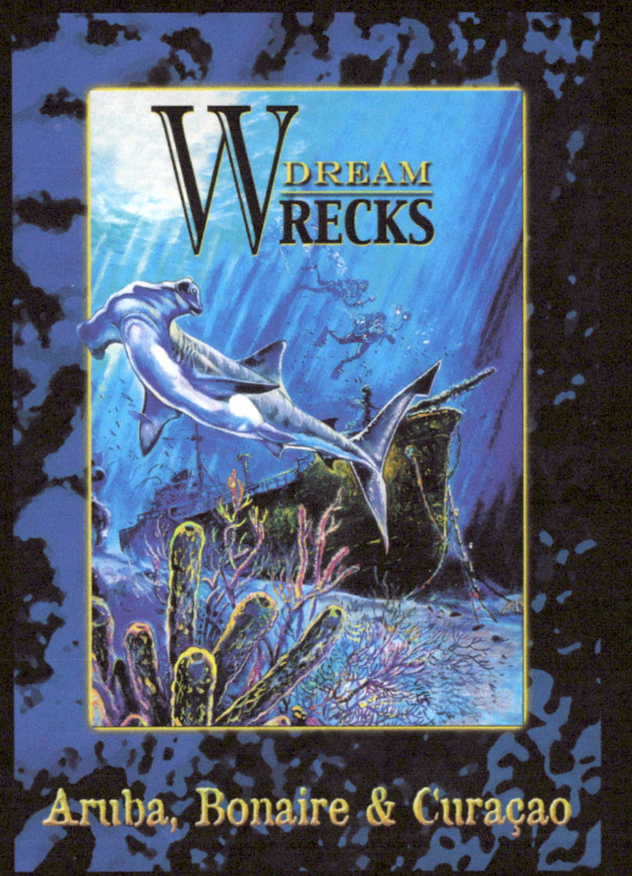

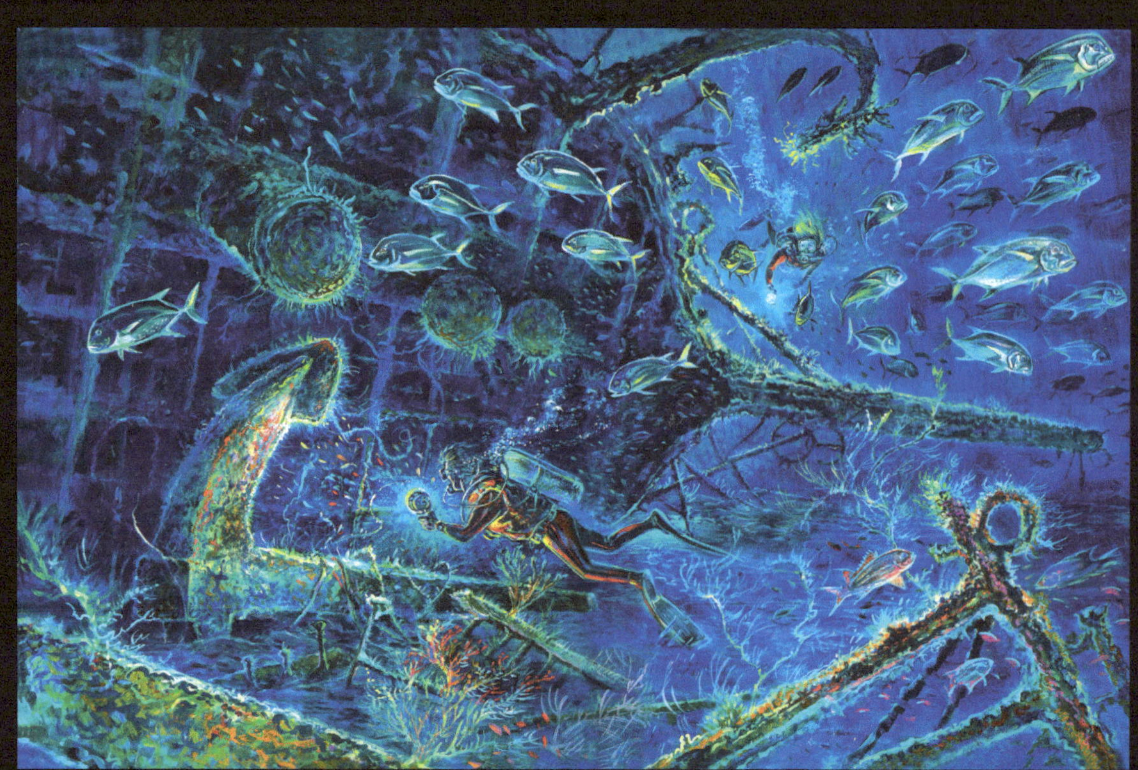

We were fascinated by the Windjammer and its beauty, with colorful coral and sponges decorated its structure. We put our photos, paintings together and we told our wreck story in the book «DreamWrecks.» This guide to the Windjammer and other shipwrecks of the Caribbean is a result of thousands of dives throughout the islands, which we visited on board my sailboat.

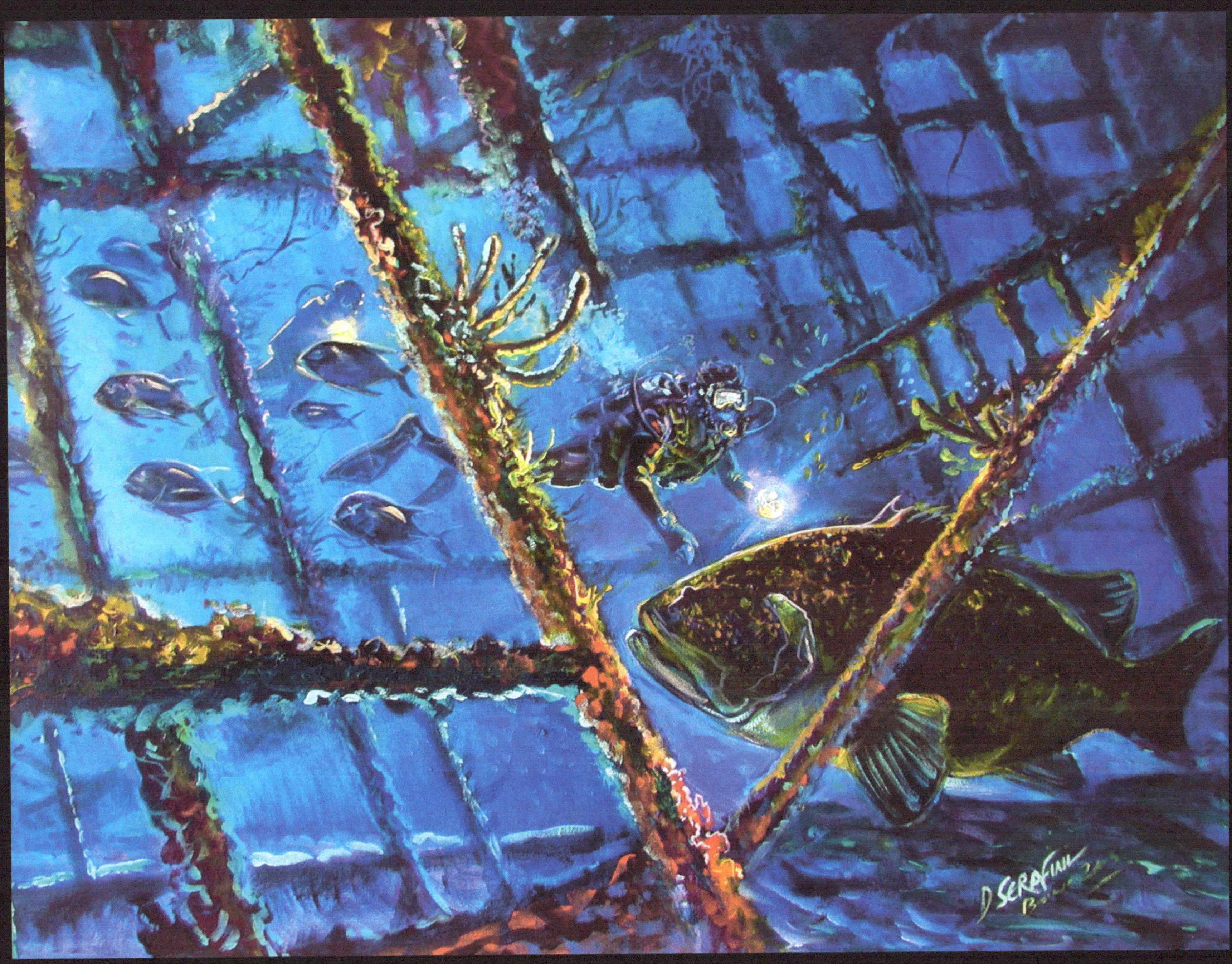

Inside the heart of the Windjammer was this gentle giant: a goliath grouper, who seemed to be keeping watch. He had his eye on us and seemed to be amused our visits.

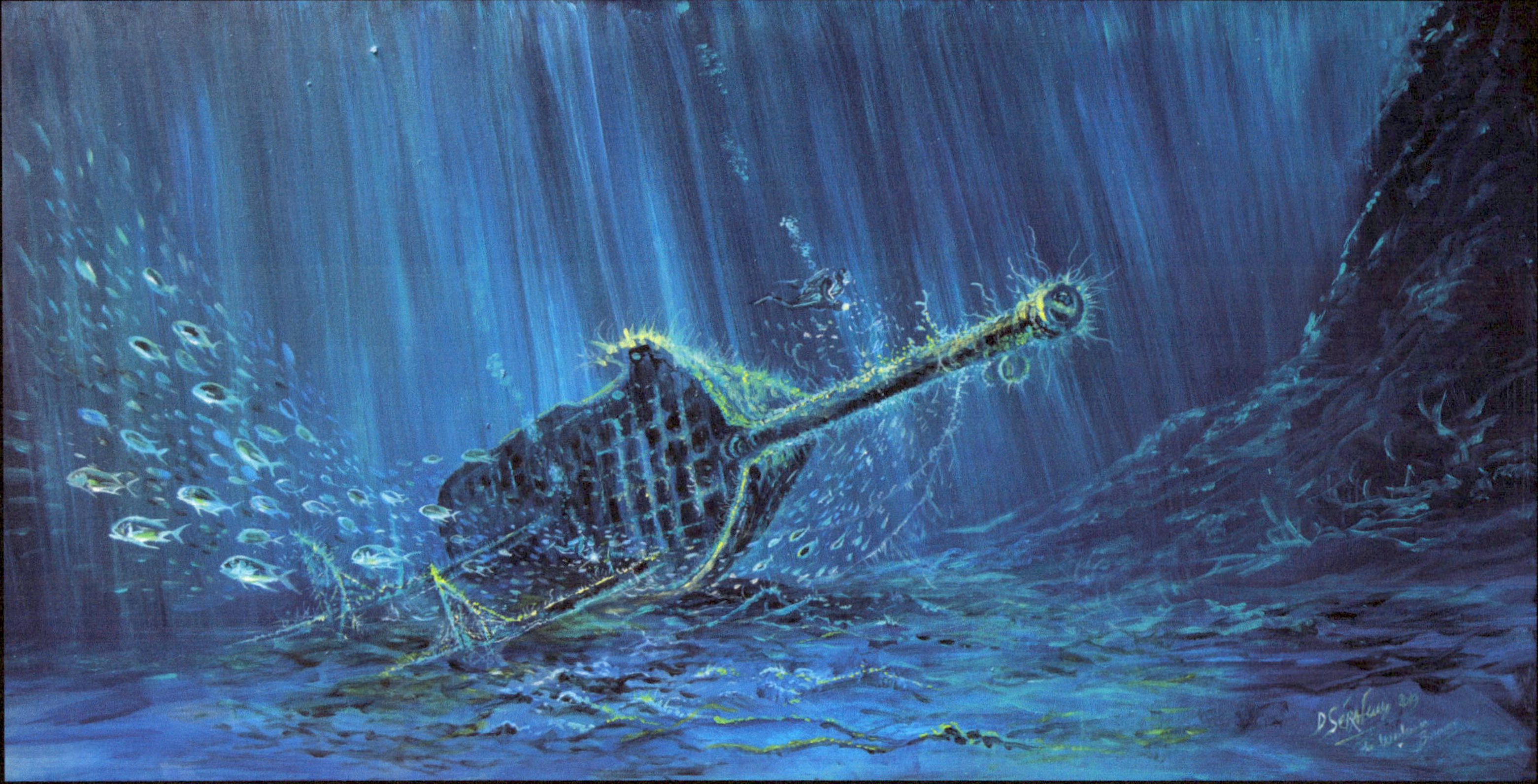

The wreck of the Windjammer inspired a whole
series of paintings, from all different angles.
The atmosphere in each painting is unique, as
most every dive on the wreck was unique.

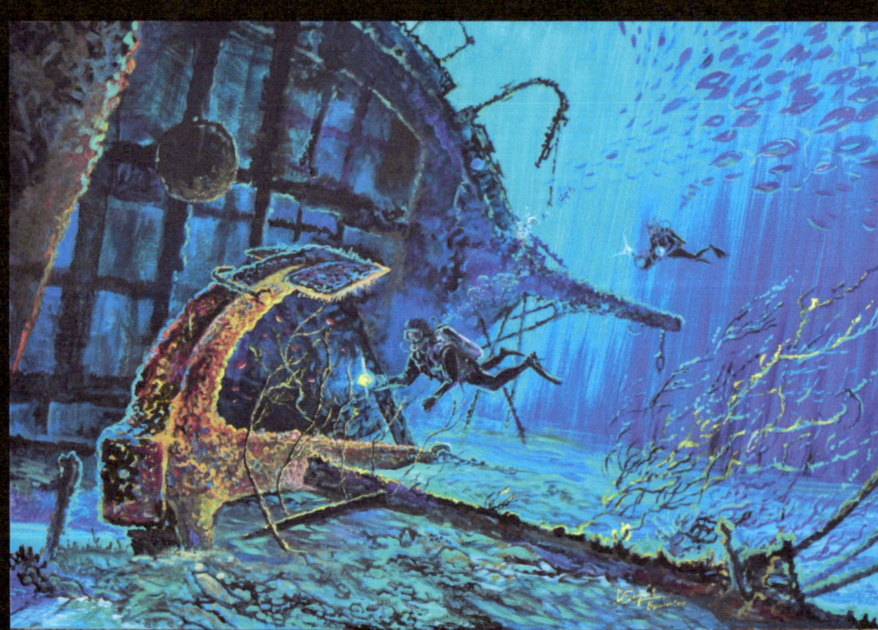

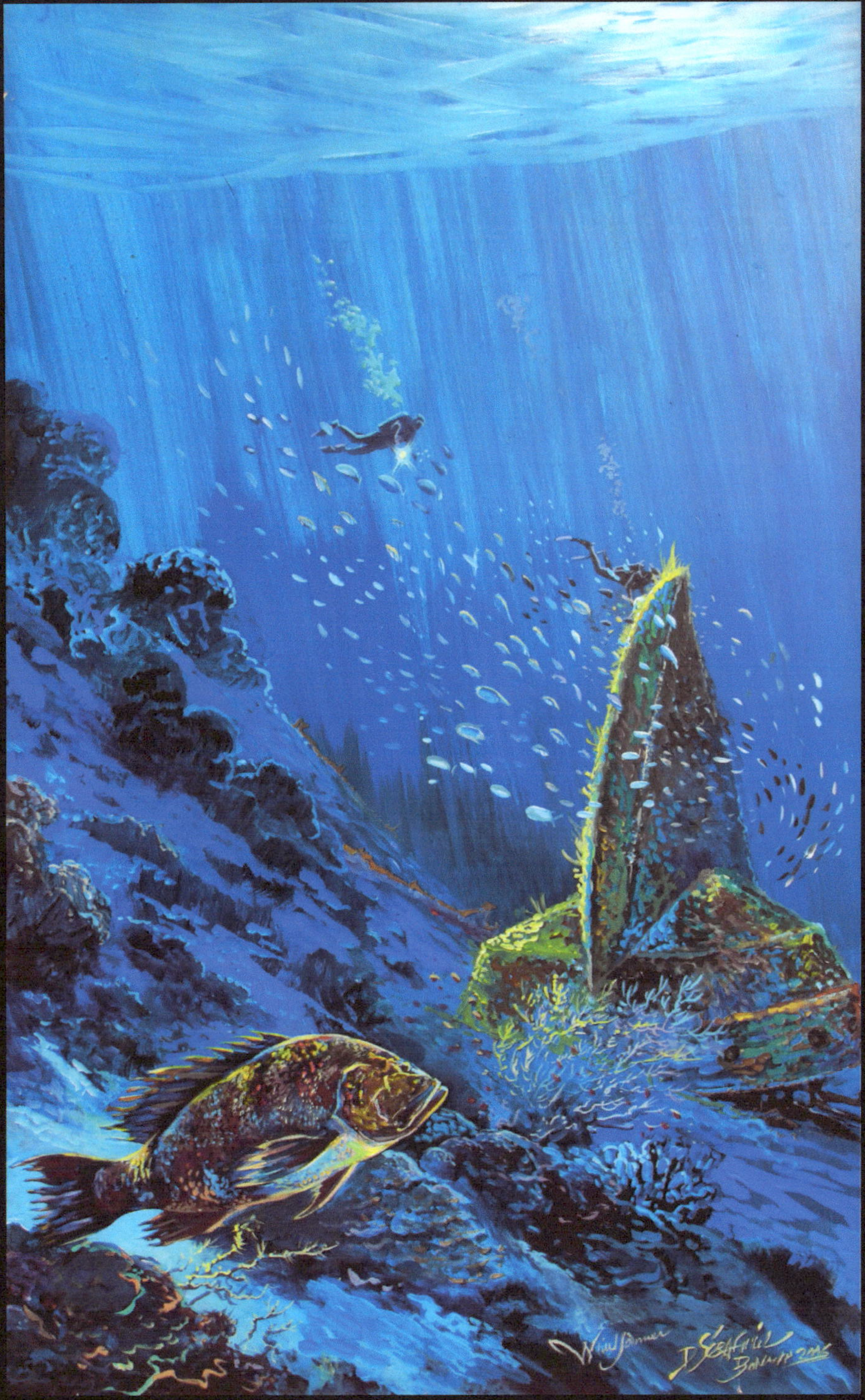

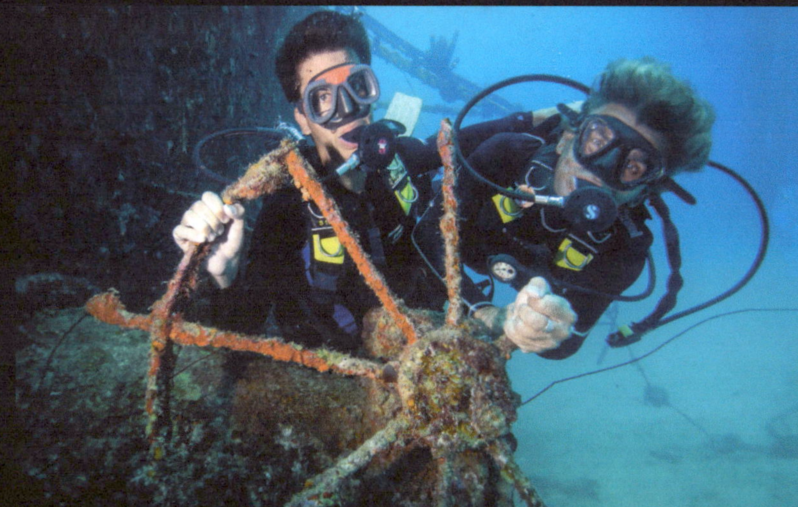

Over time, wrecks collapse and disappear, digested by the sea. In 2005 the Windjammer changed. Its hull flipped over and the keel pointed towards the surface.

My son Enzo has accompanied me on many of my dives. It is a pleasure to be able to share my passion with him and my other children.

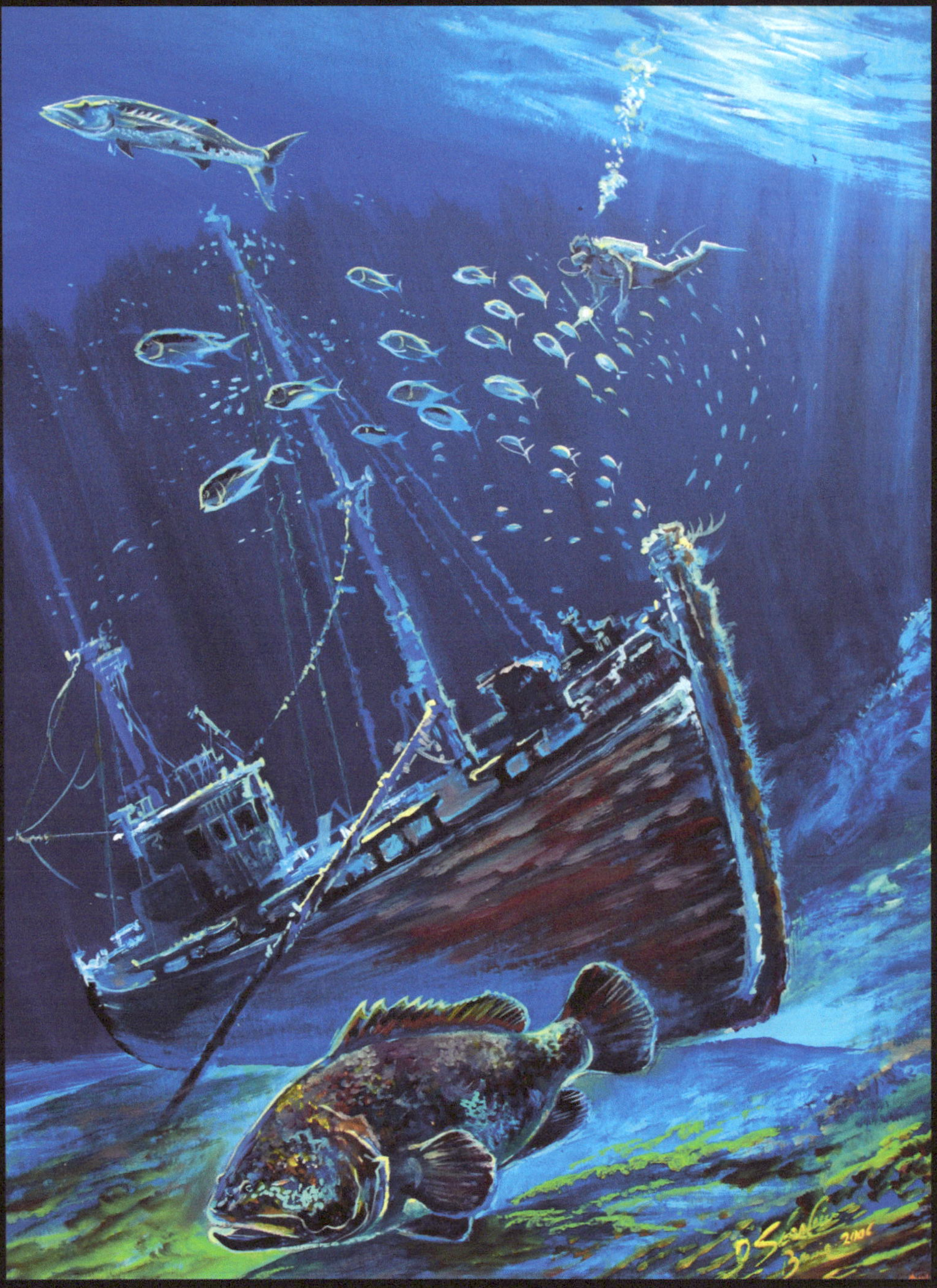

One day in 2004, Our Confidence, a wooden sailboat, sank while leaving the marina in Bonaire. Soon after, the wreck became a hunting ground for a young goliath grouper.

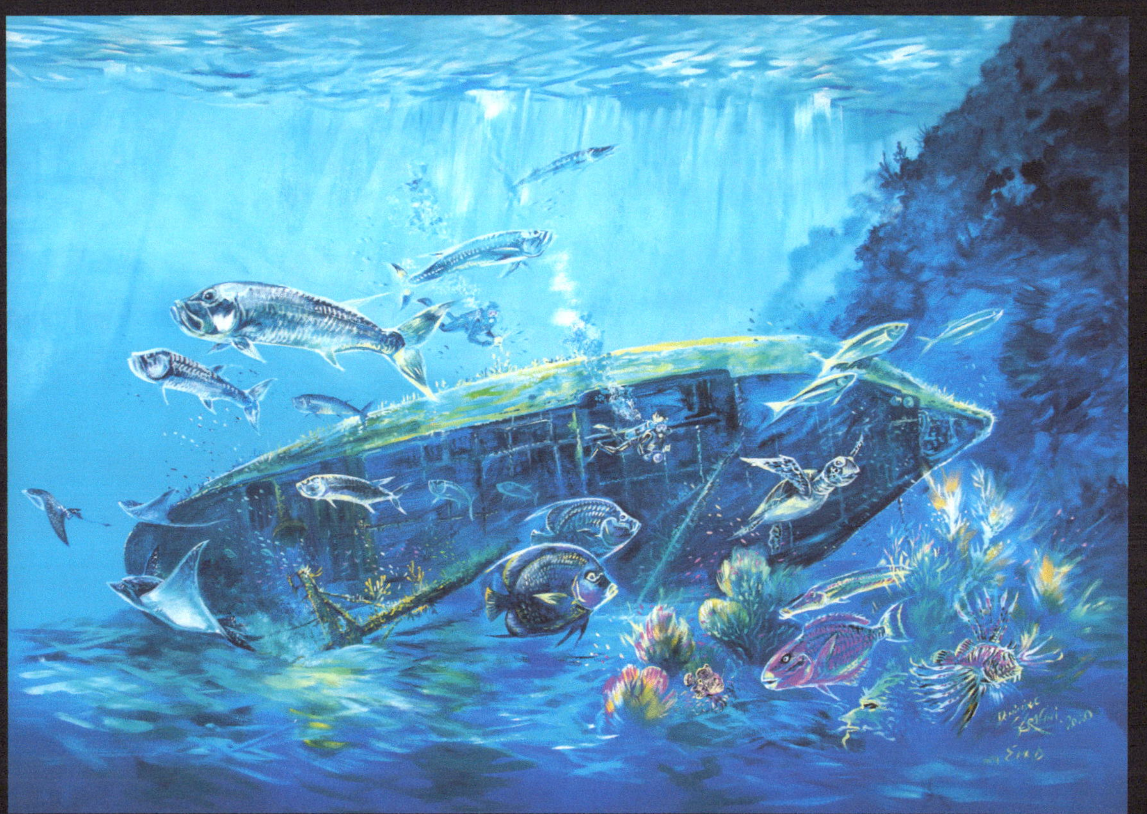

The most famous wreck of Bonaire is without a doubt the Hilma Hooker. This old freighter was sunk as an artificial reef for the pleasure of divers. This wreck has inspired several paintings, all celebrating its beauty.

In 2020, I did a large mural of the Hilma Hooker for my friend Bart and his Windsock dive center called WannaDive.

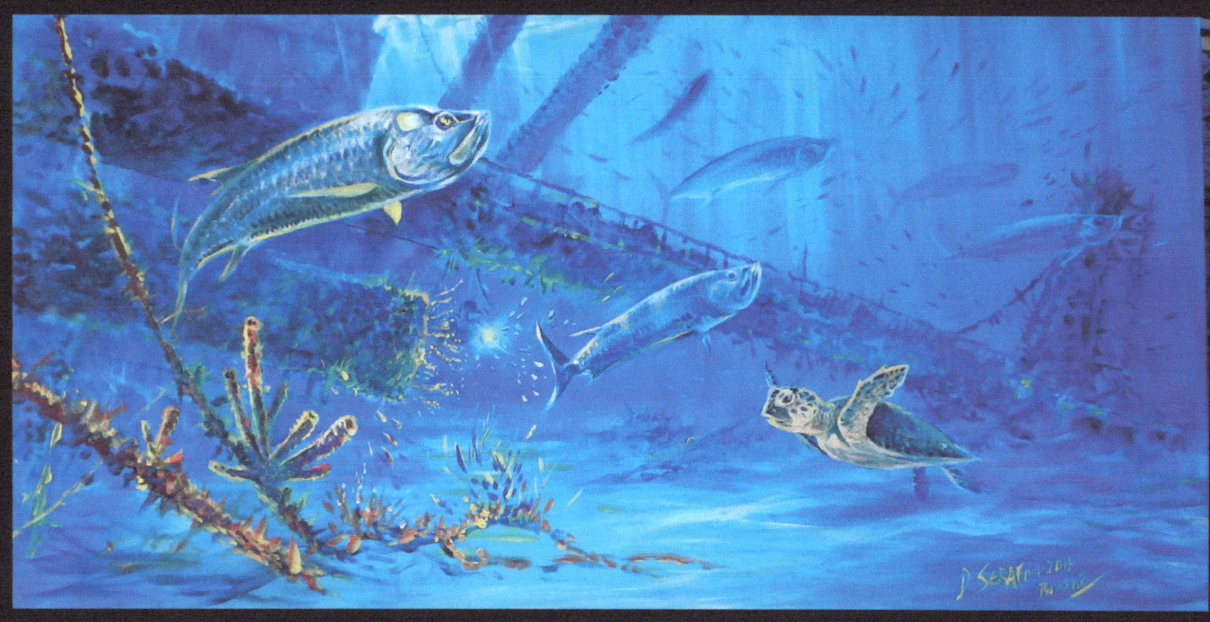

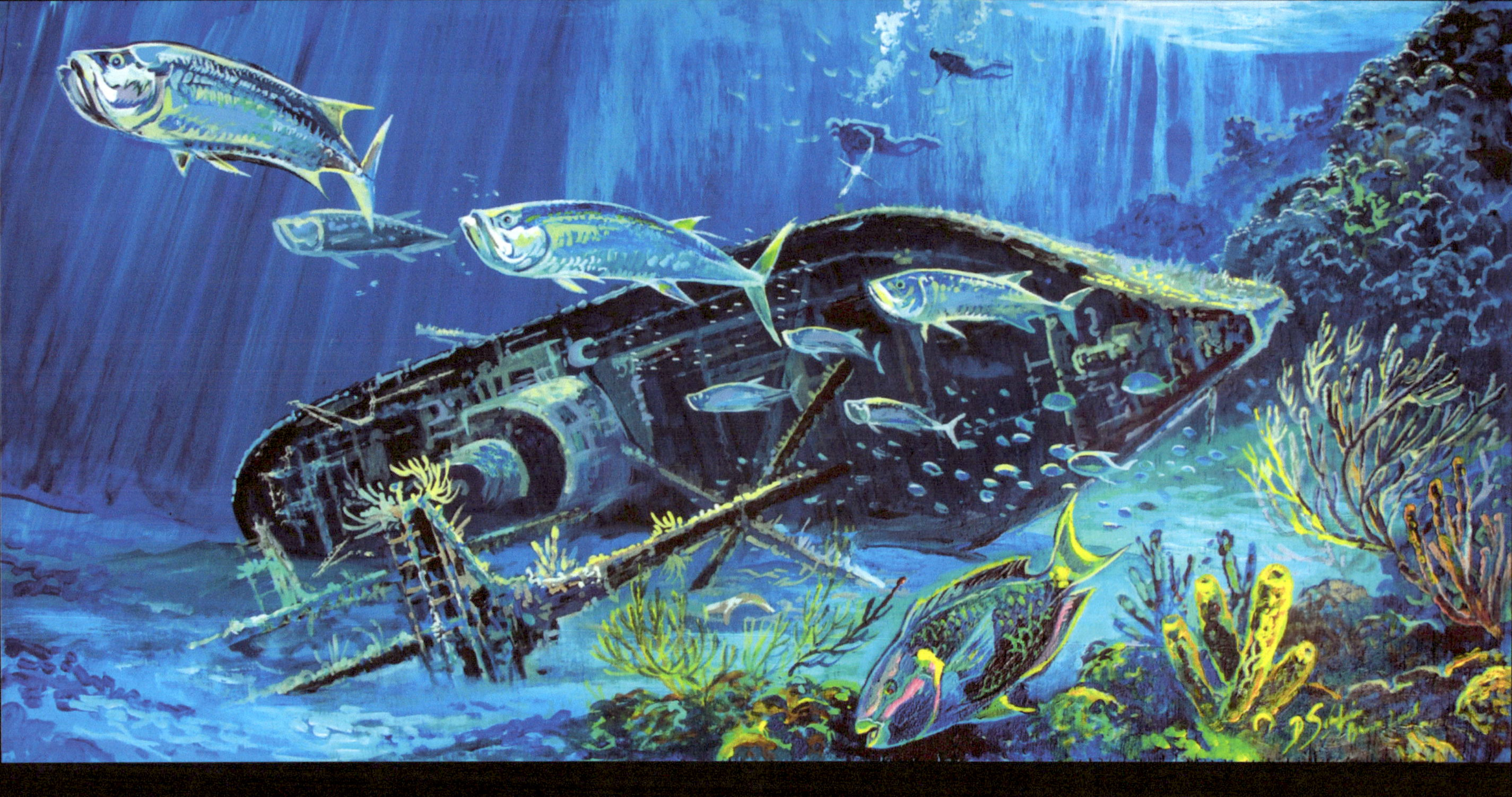

The Hilma Hooker, illegally transporting contraband, was seized by the police and later sunk. A group of tarpons quickly chose the wreck as their home. They hunt schools of small fish that hide in the cargo hulls.

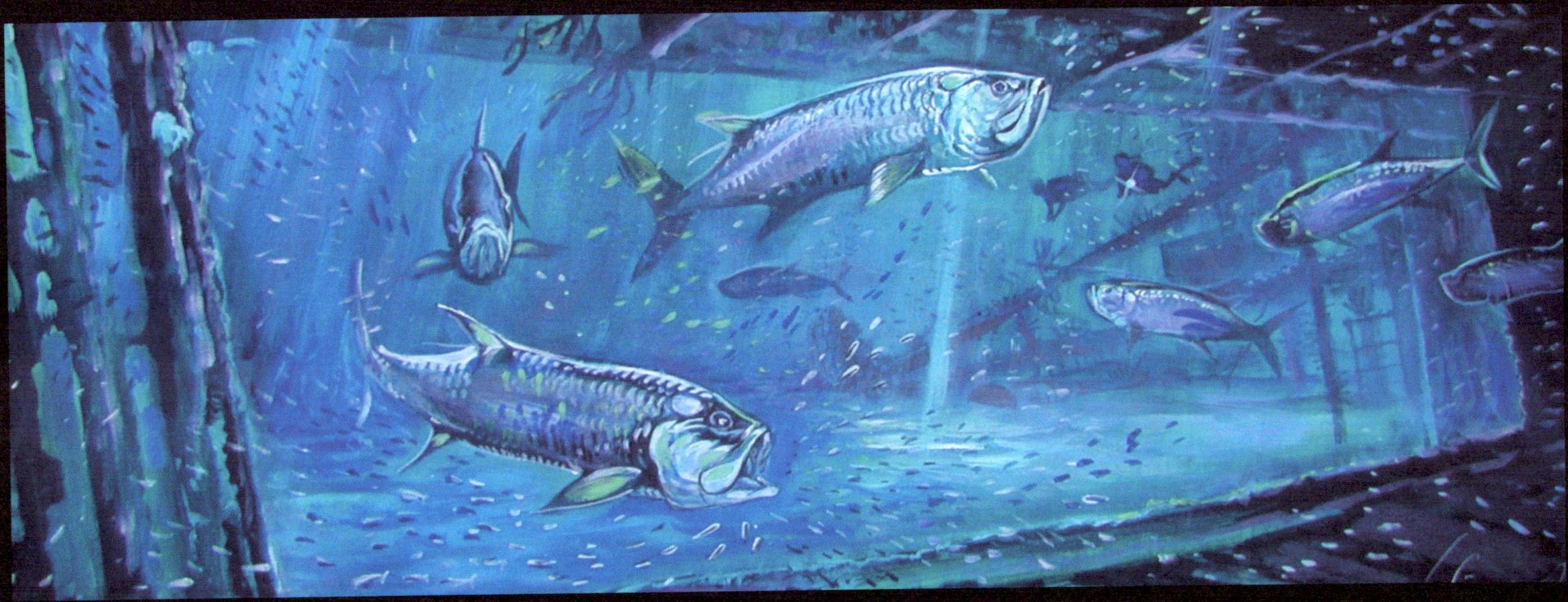

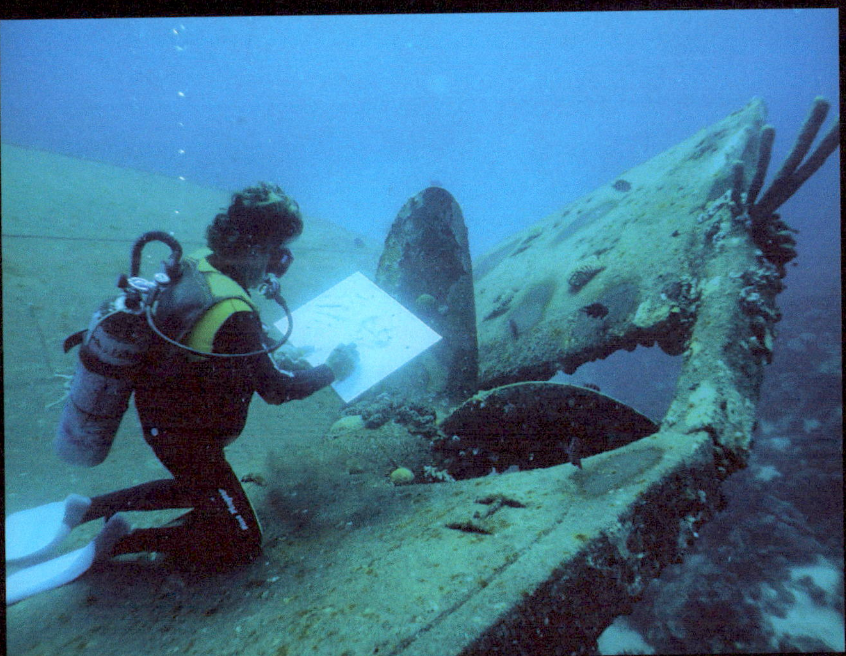
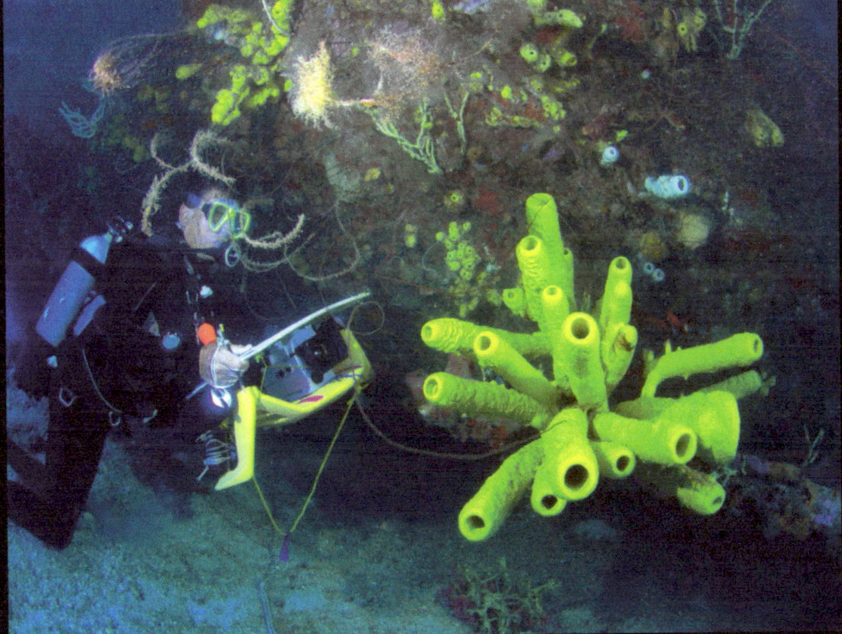

To draw underwater, I use a piece of white plastic and a grease pencil. I quietly sit on the sandy bottom or on a wreck and make my sketch. Often curious fish will come by and take a long look at me. Back on land, I create my painting from these sketches as well as my memory of the dive.

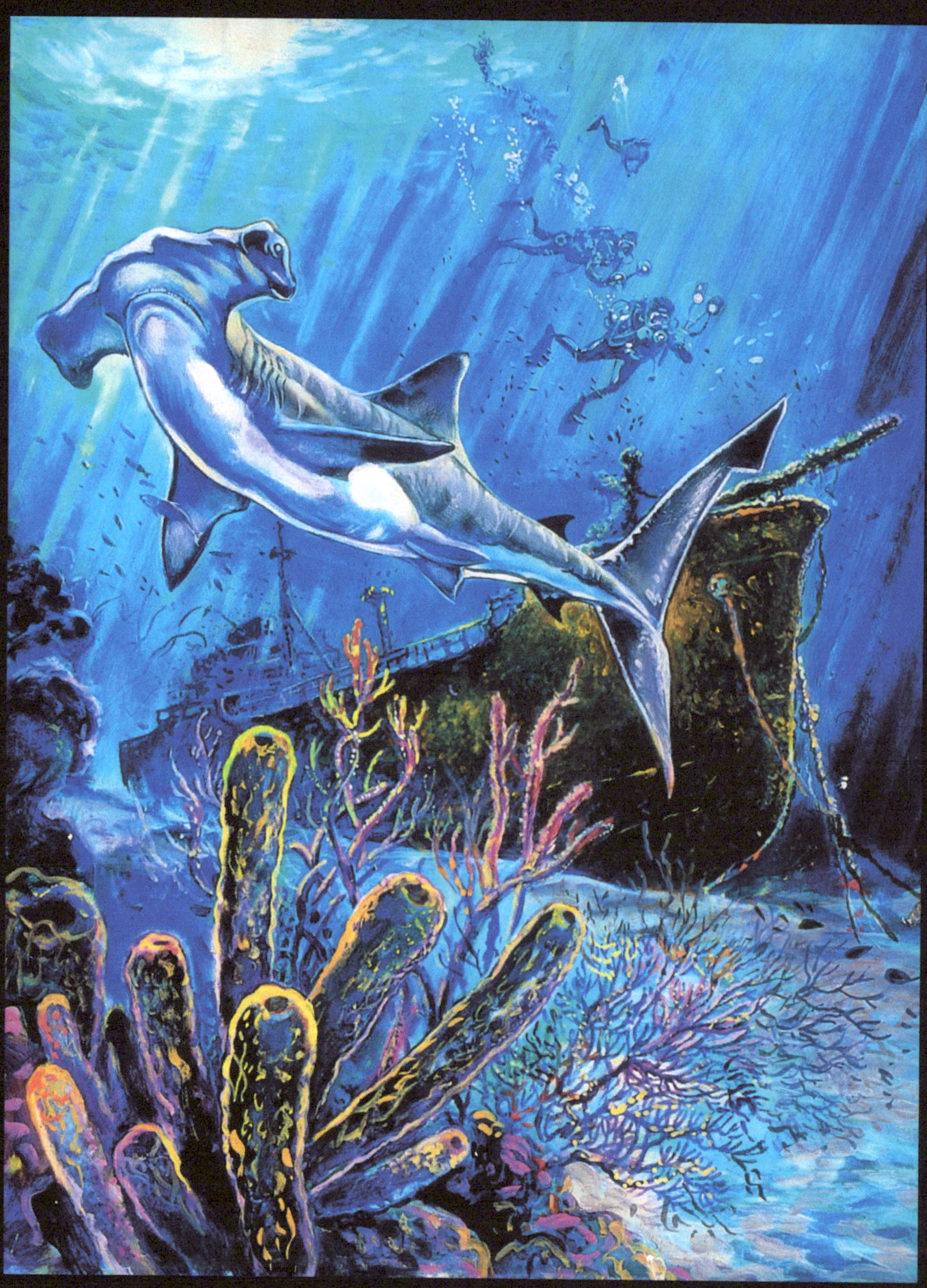

Over time, shipwrecks become marine sanctuaries where barracudas, turtles, rays congregate.
One day, on the wreck of the Superior Producer in Curaçao, a hammerhead shark swam by overhead.

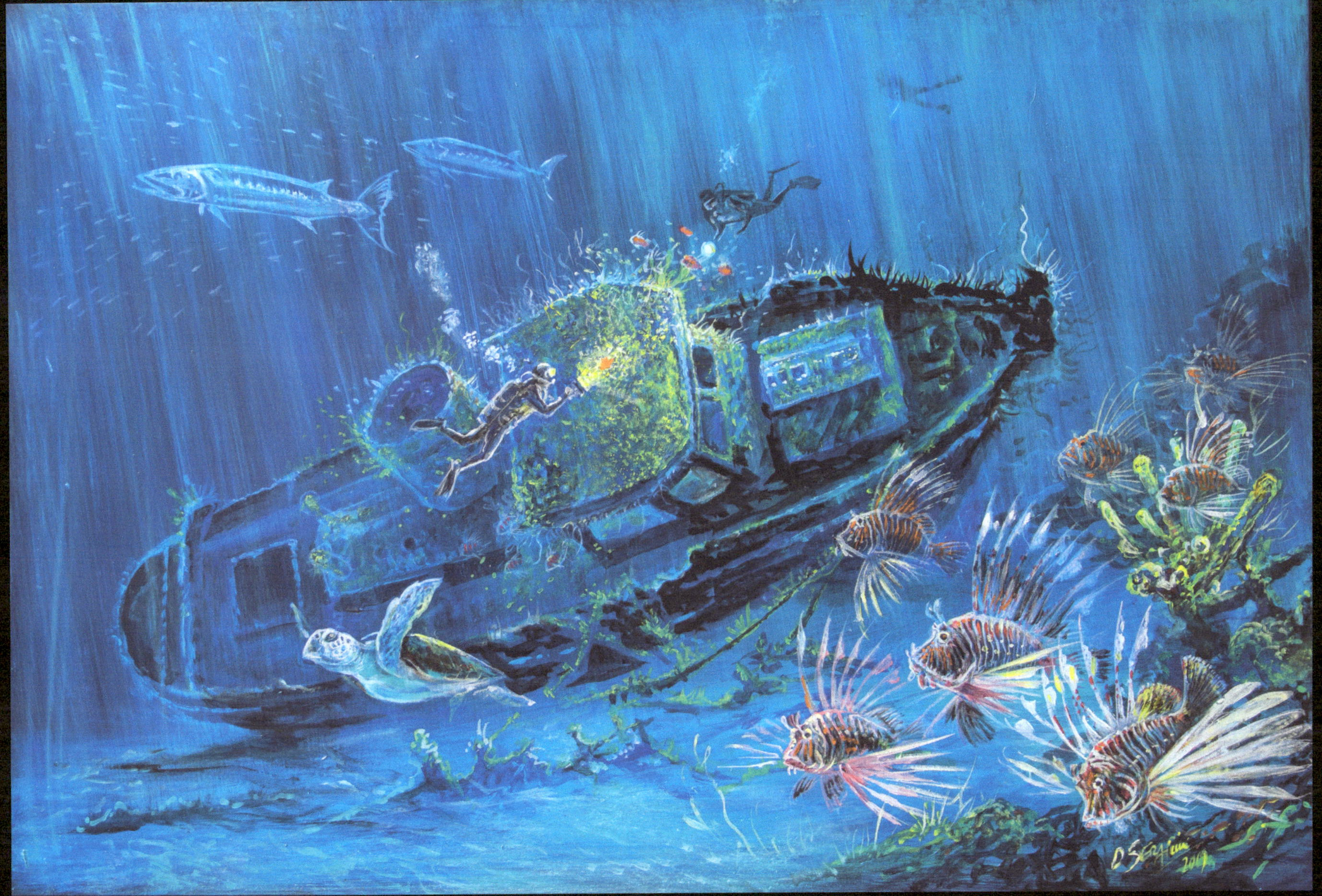

In the 1960s in Curaçao, cars were thrown into the sea - a very non-ecological way of disposing of old vehicles. While hauling cars out to sink, this large tugboat capsized and sank in 165 feet of water in Vaersen Bay. Too deep for most recreational divers, the shipwreck is a quiet and well appreciated home for groups of lionfish.

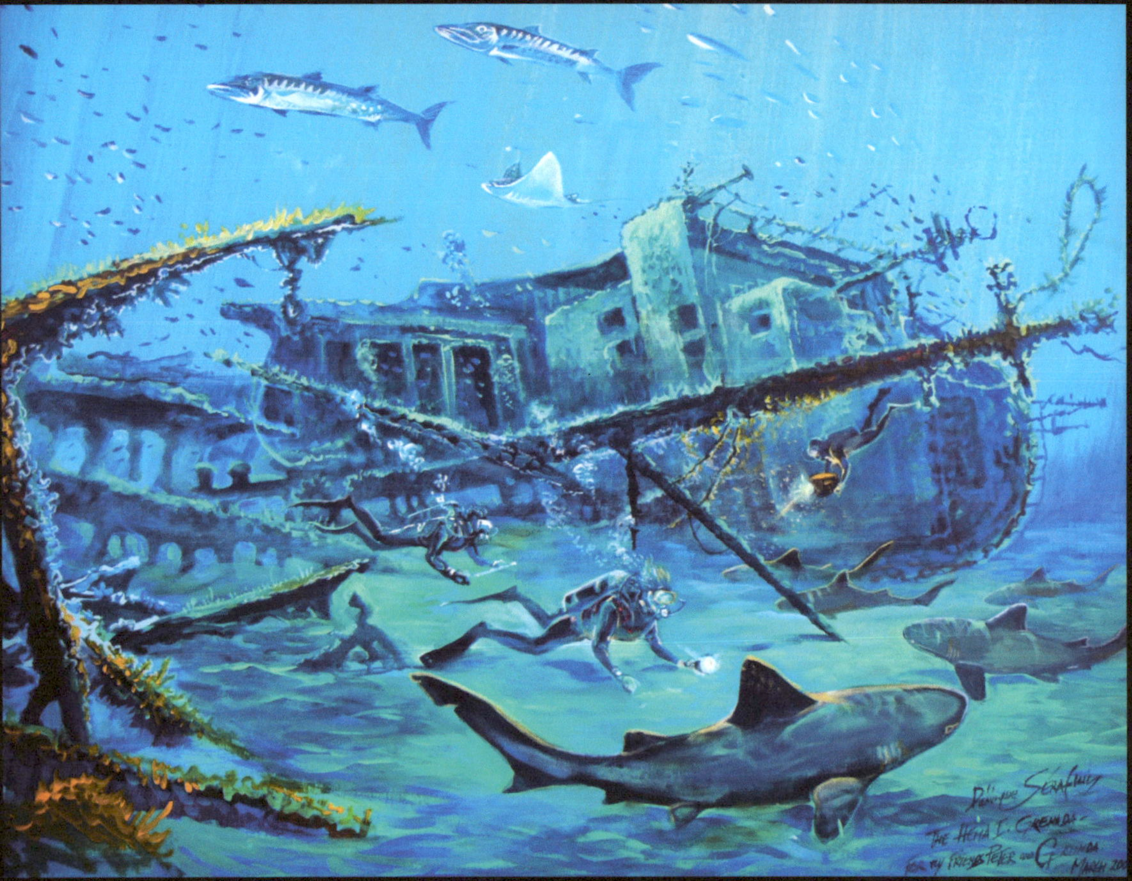

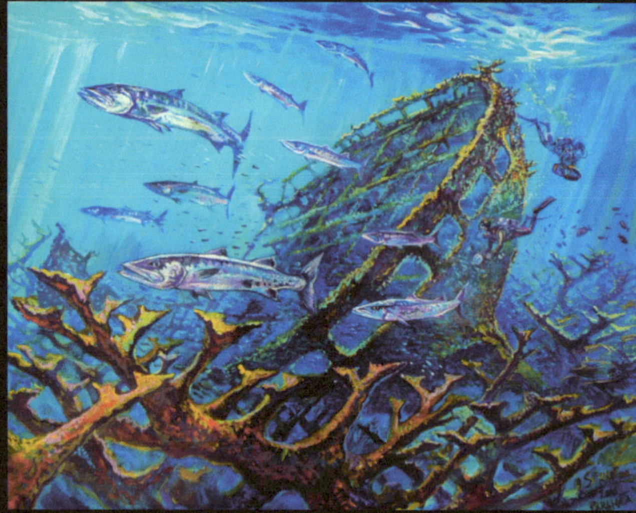

Between Grenada and Trinidad, far from the coast, many freighters, like the Hema 1 have sunk, victims of mechanical problems as well as hurricanes.

In the British Virgin Islands, the Paramatta, a side-wheel steamer, wrecked on Anegada Horseshoe Reef on its first trans-Atlantic trip.

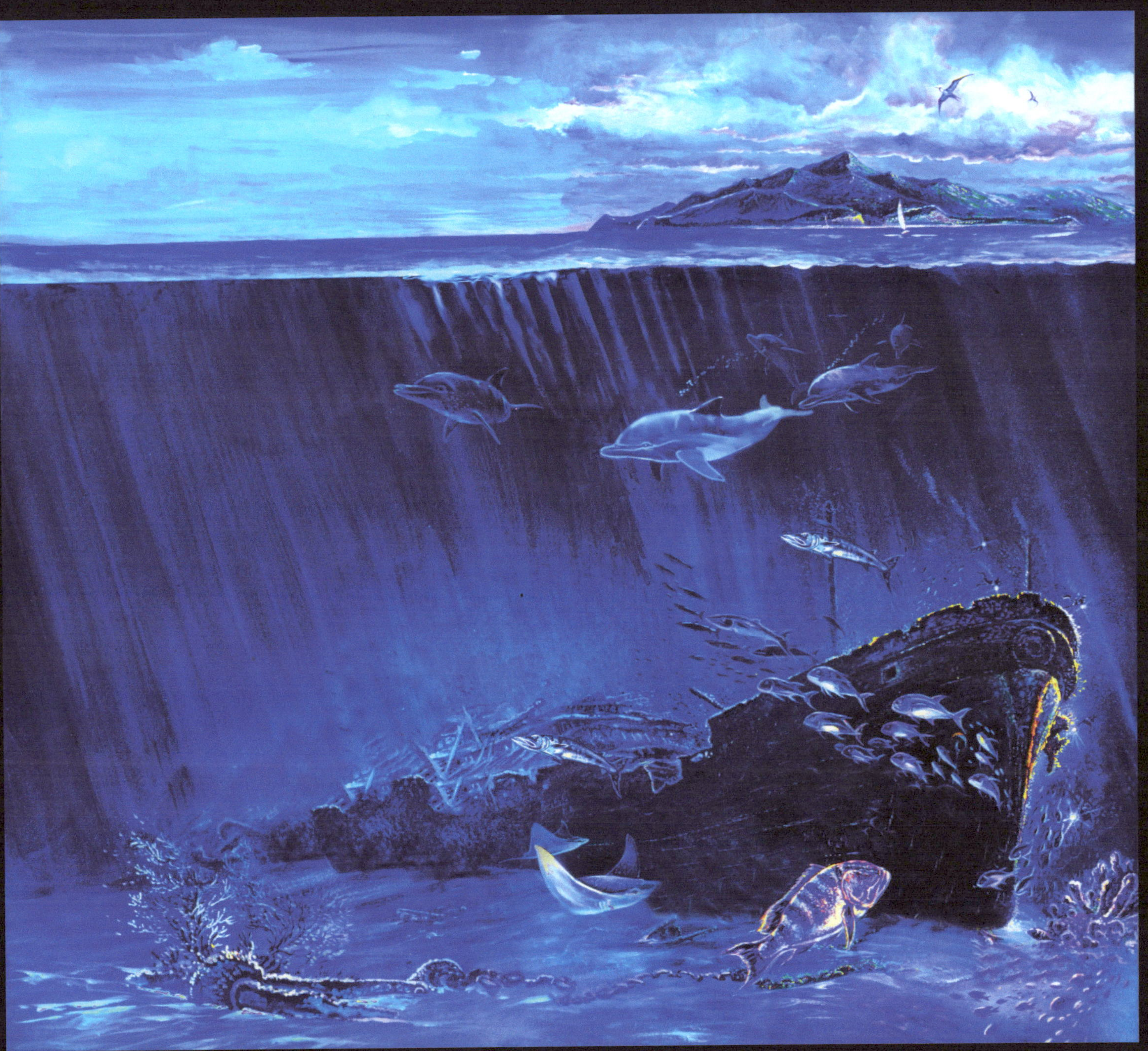

The Bianca C is known by divers as the Titanic of the Caribbean. In 1960, this cruise ship caught fire in Saint George's harbor, Grenada. This enormous wreck is over 330 feet long and is an exceptional dive.

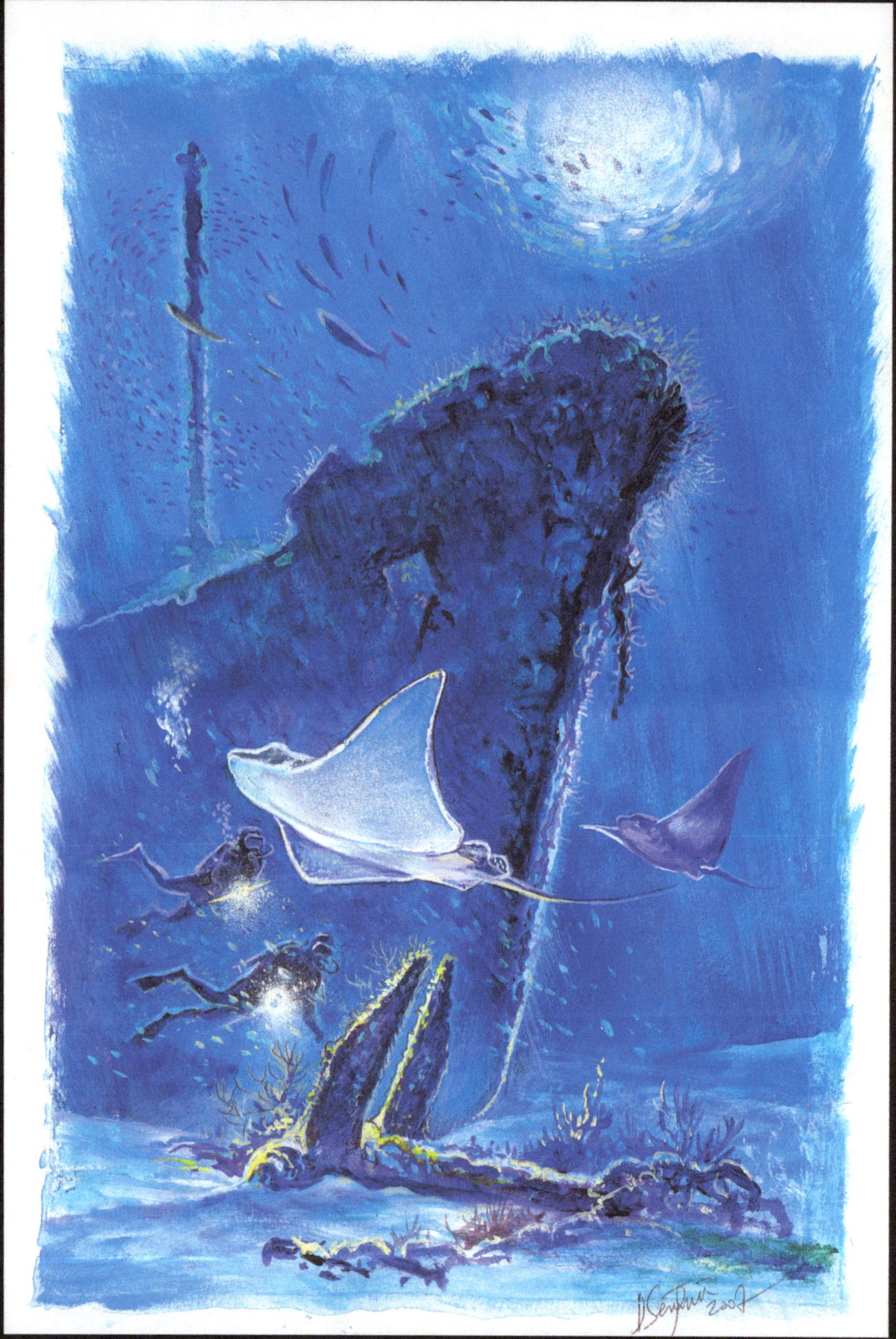

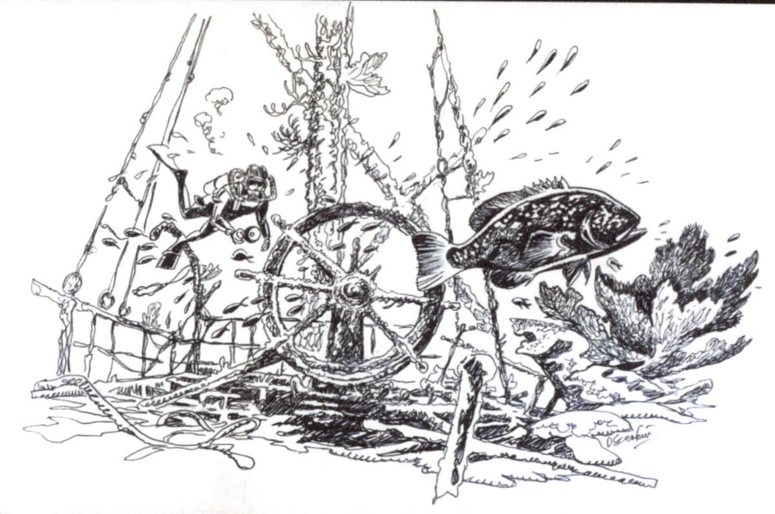

An ideal angle for a sketch of the Bianca C is at the foot of the bow, in 200 feet of water near the anchor. On a lucky day, you can see eagle rays passing in the blue. From my underwater pencil sketches, I later made this painting back on land.

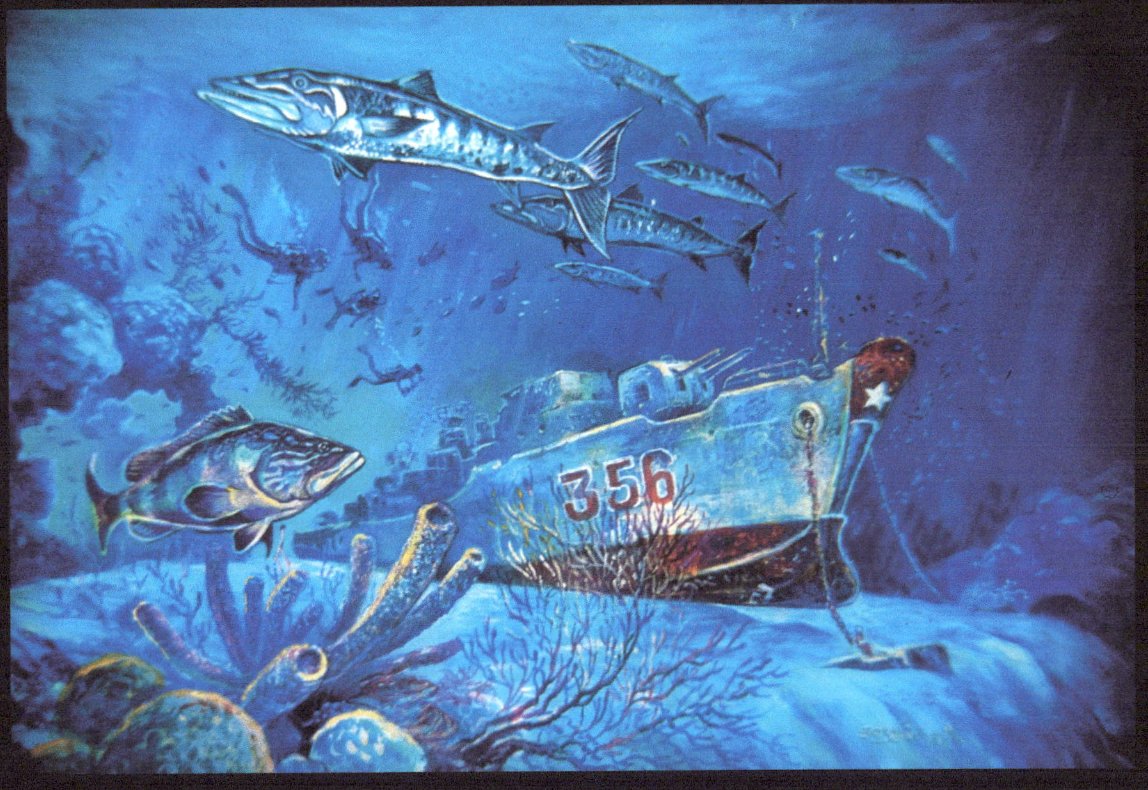

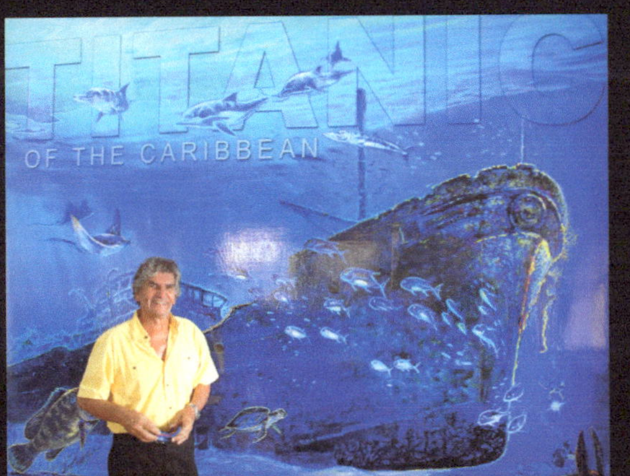

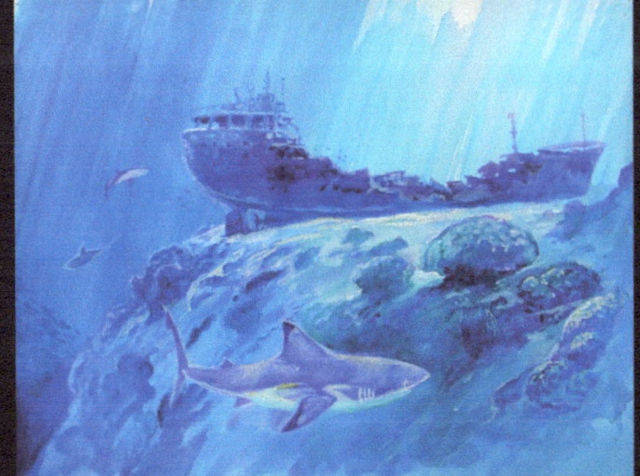

During the filming of the tv series «DreamWrecks» we explored the most spectacular shipwrecks of the Caribbean... Cayman Islands, Bahamas, Roatan, Grenada, Aruba, Curaçao...

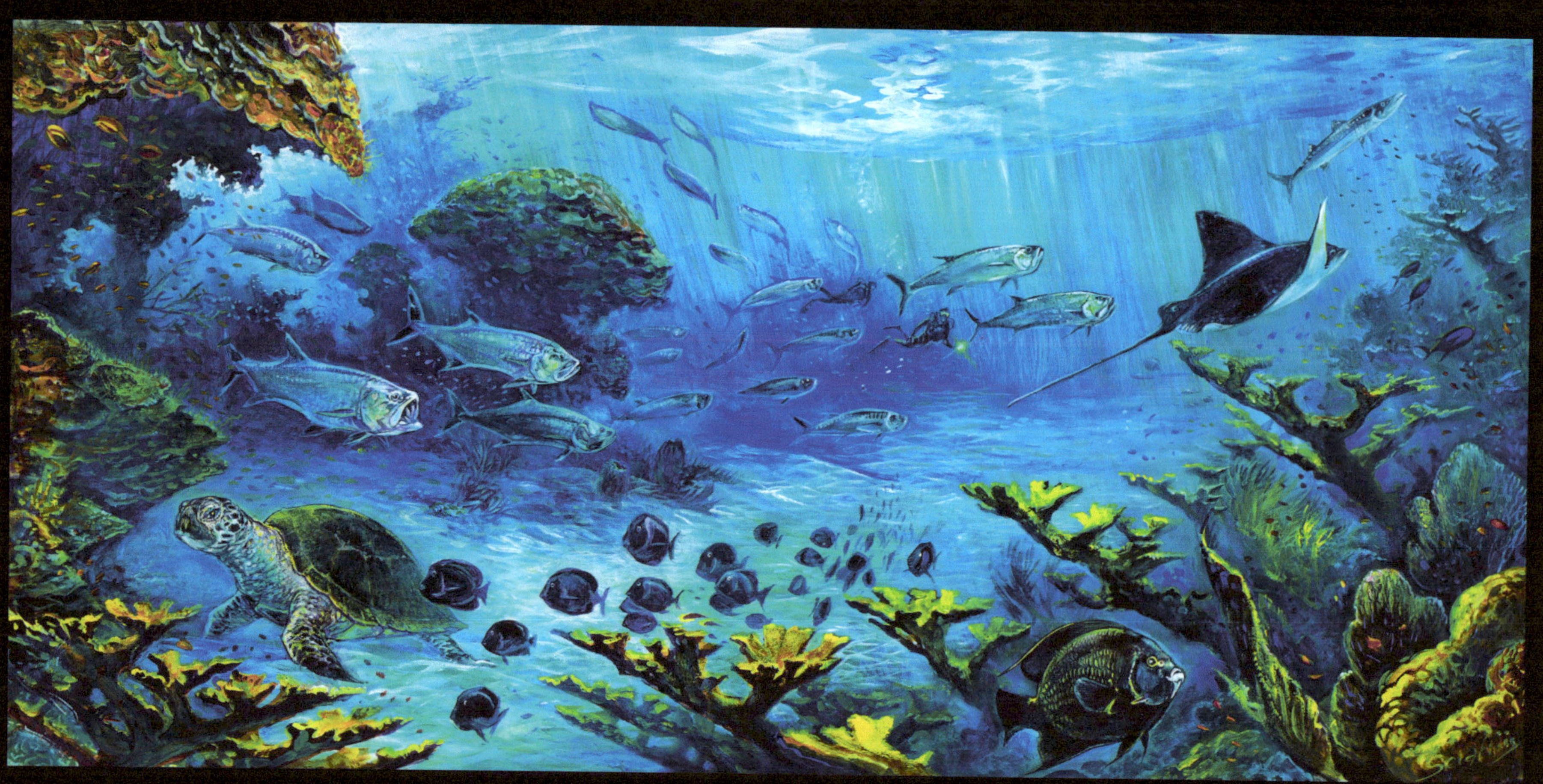

Coral reefs are living treasures with infinite shapes and colors. They are also very complex and fragile ecosystems. During my dives around our blue planet, I have unfortunately witnessed their destruction. Pollution, plastic waste and global warming threaten the survival of reefs.

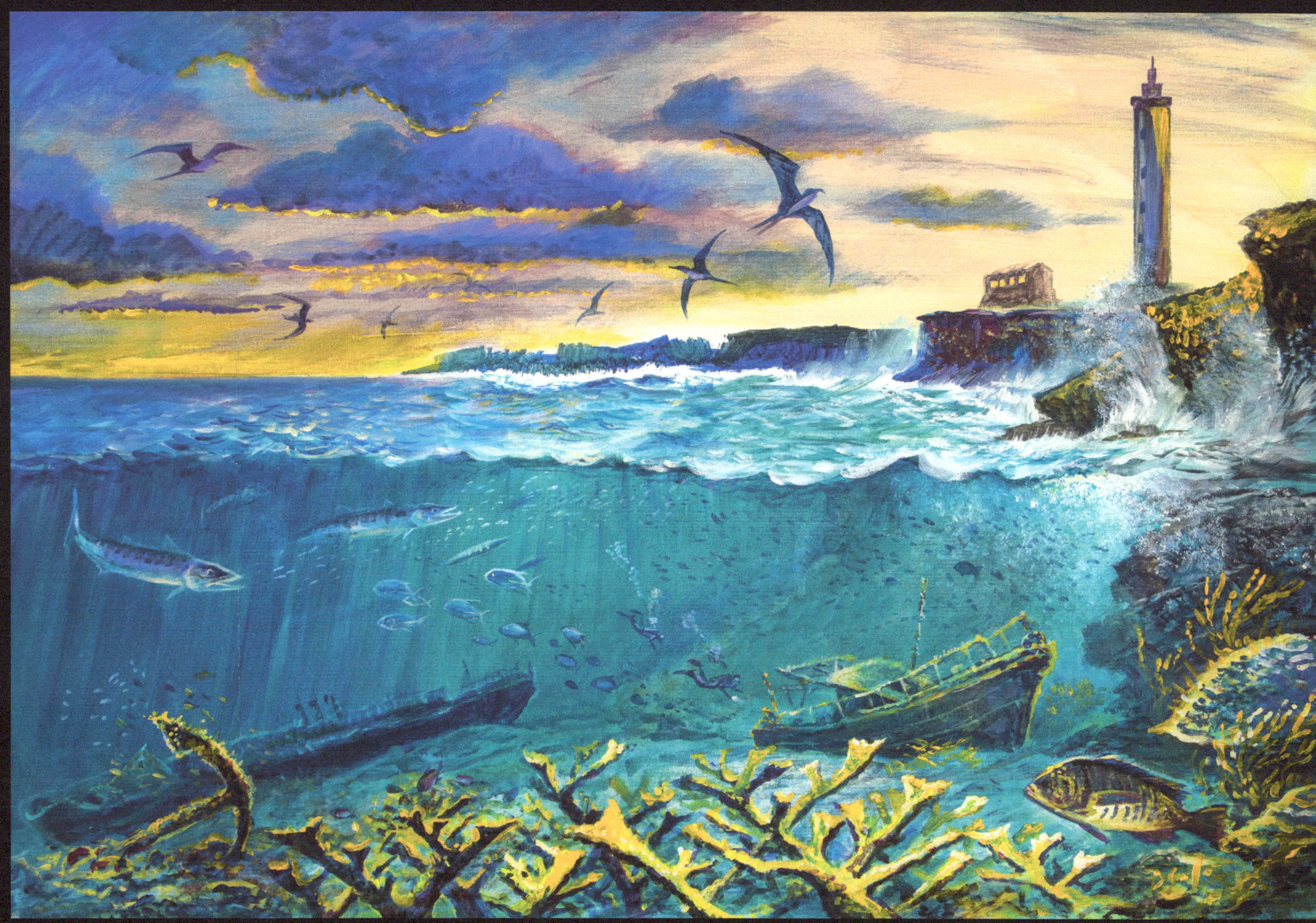

A handful of shipwrecks are at the base of the Spelonk lighthouse on the windward side of Bonaire. This painting was inspired by the dramatic atmosphere that prevails, with huge waves beating down on the rocky cliffs.

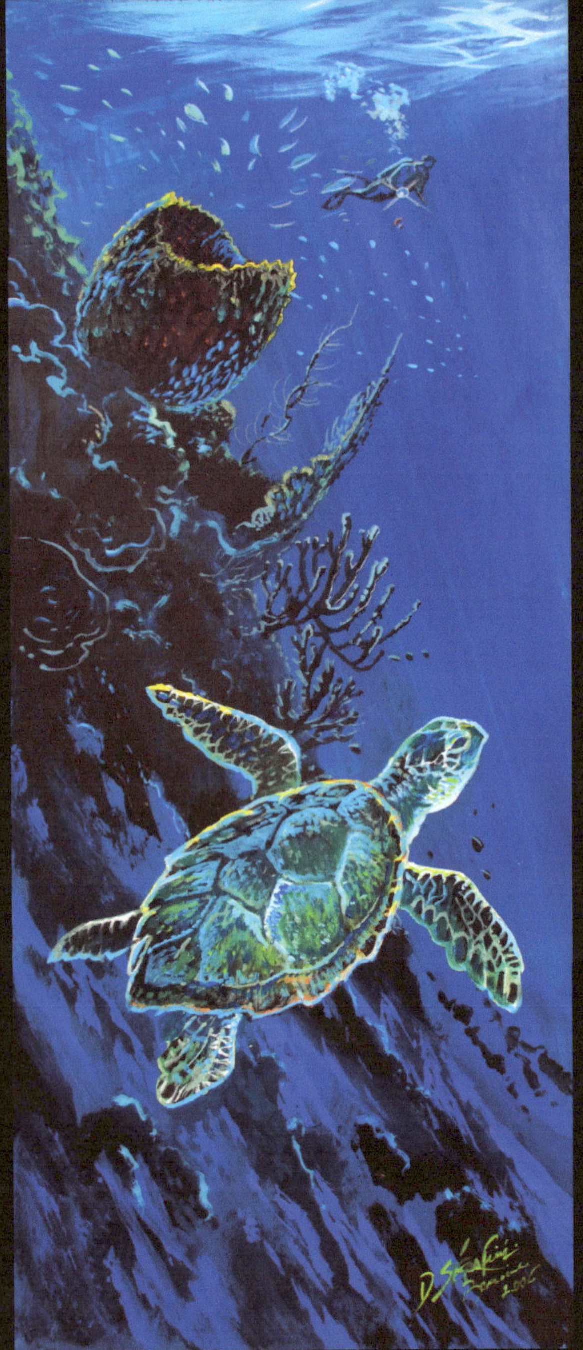
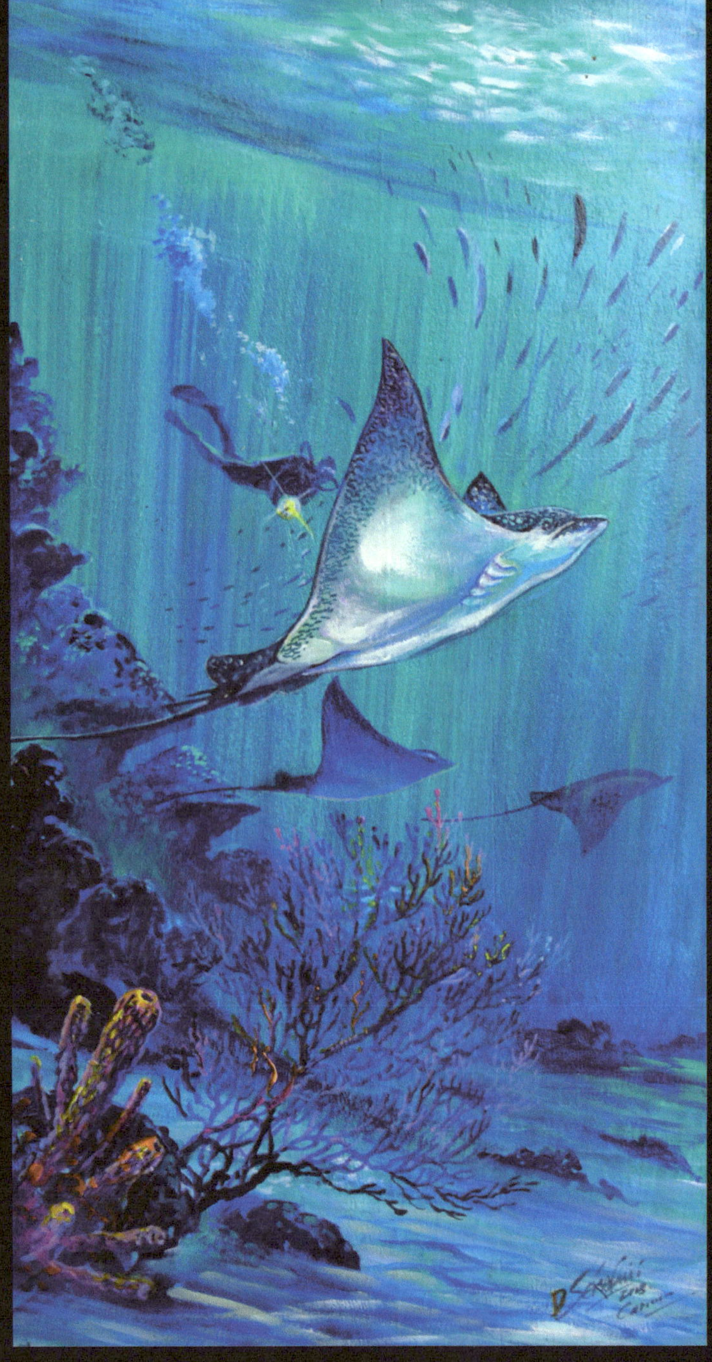

Coral reefs are home to millions of living creatures. From the smallest coral polyp to the largest shark, each depend on the other for its survival, predator or prey. In this underwater world, humans are simply visitors, watching but not touching.

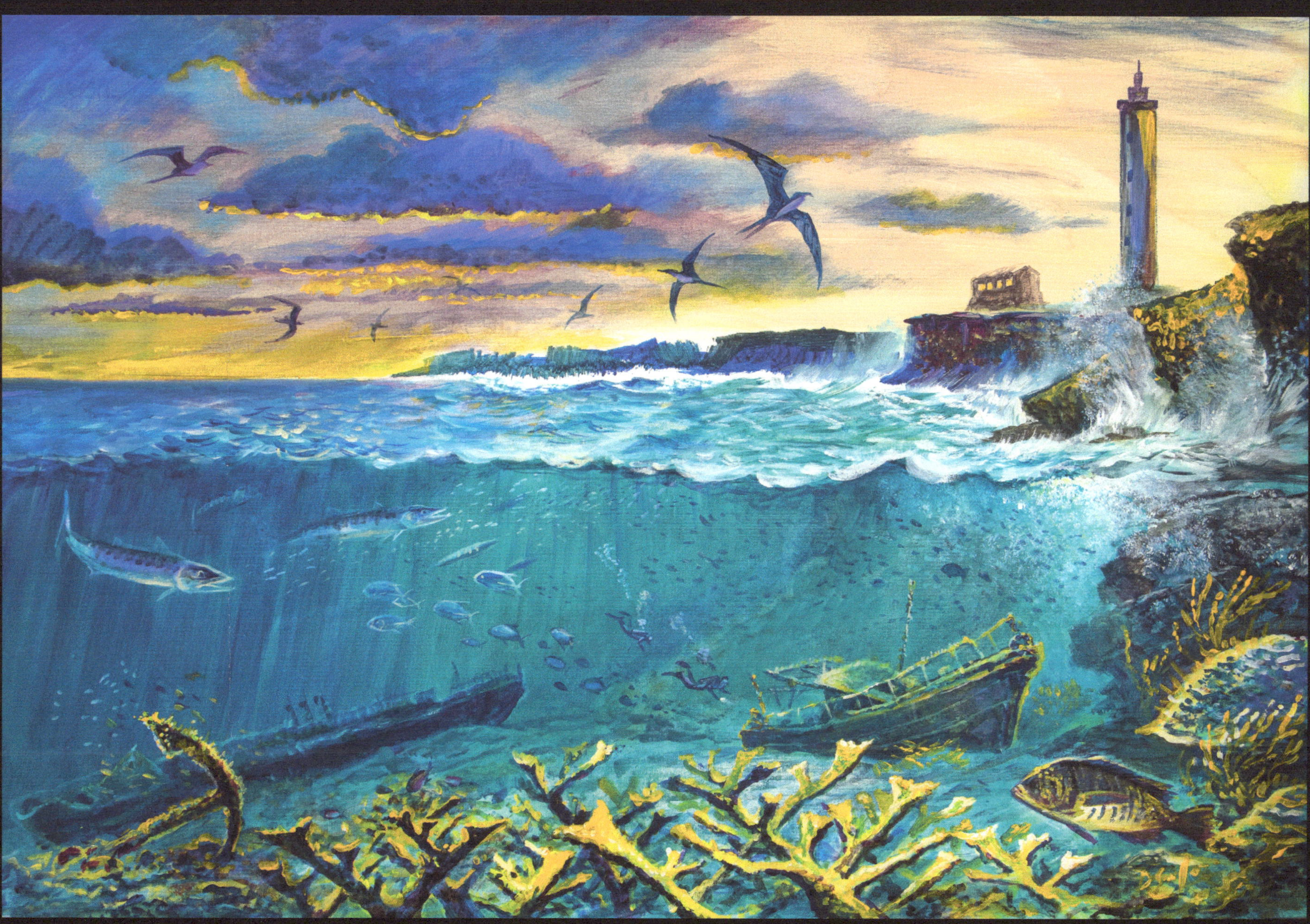

A handful of shipwrecks are at the base of the Spelonk lighthouse on the windward side of Bonaire. This painting was inspired by the dramatic atmosphere that prevails, with huge waves beating down on the rocky cliffs.

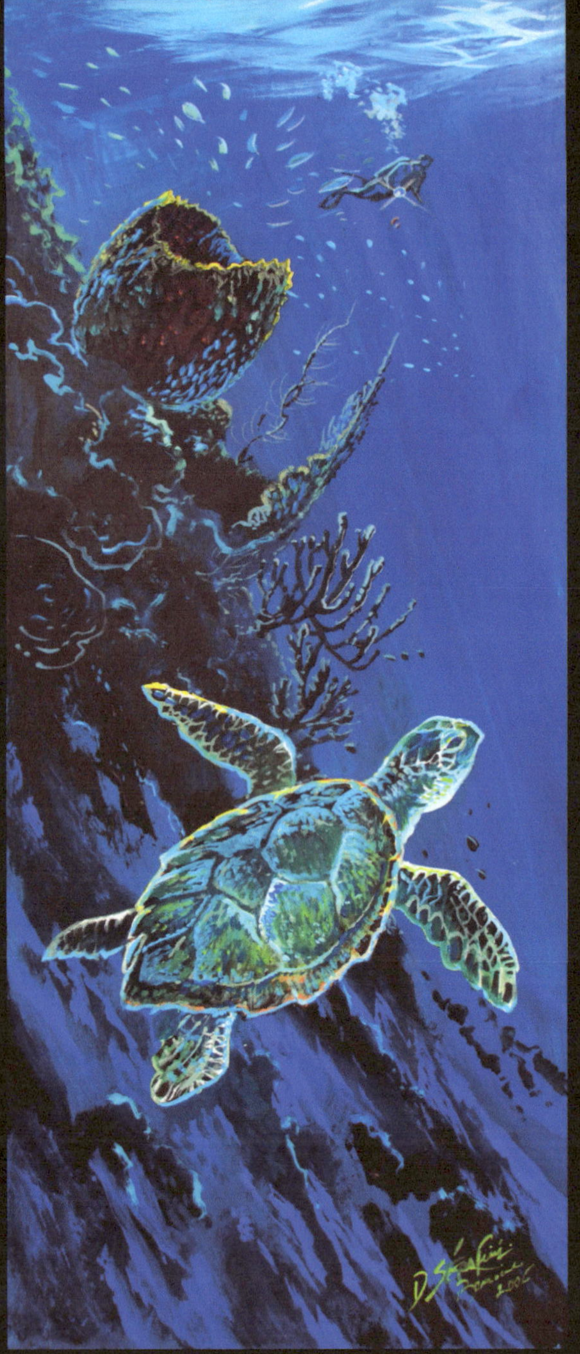
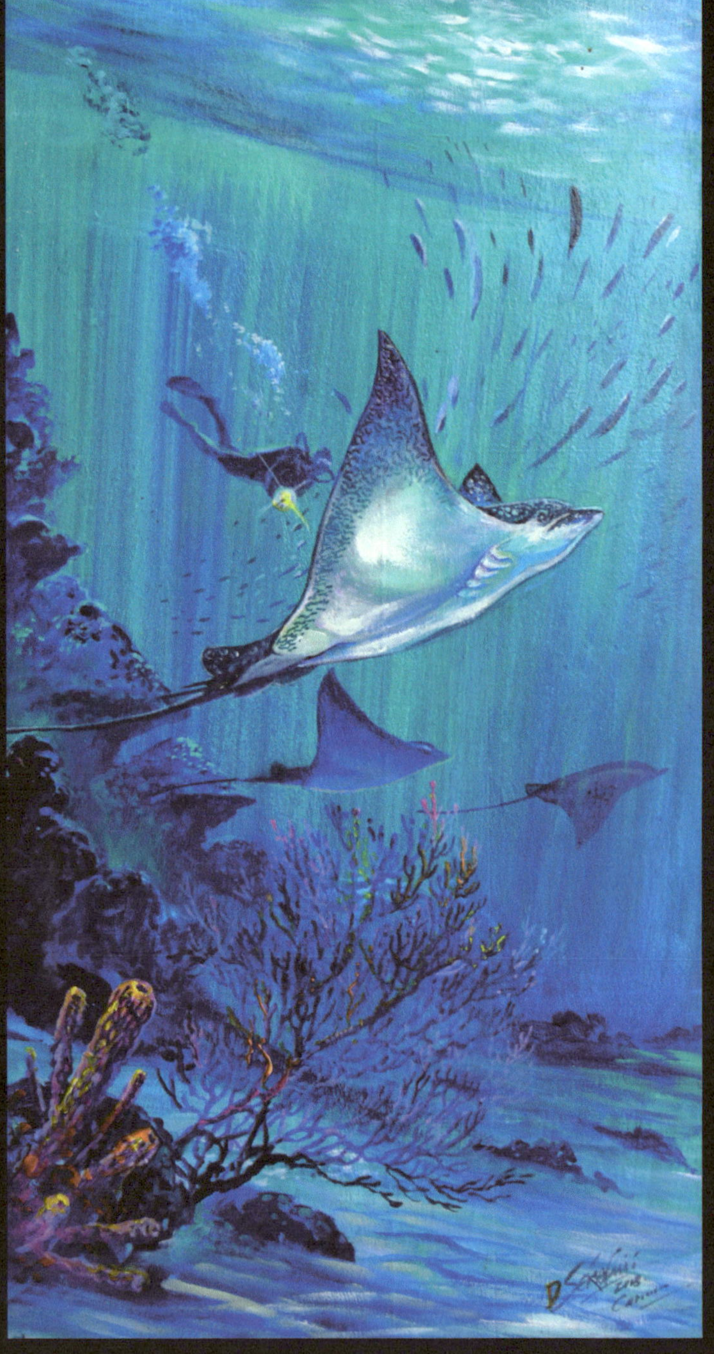

Coral reefs are home to millions of living creatures. From the smallest coral polyp to the largest shark, each depend on the other for its survival, predator or prey. In this underwater world, humans are simply visitors, watching but not touching.

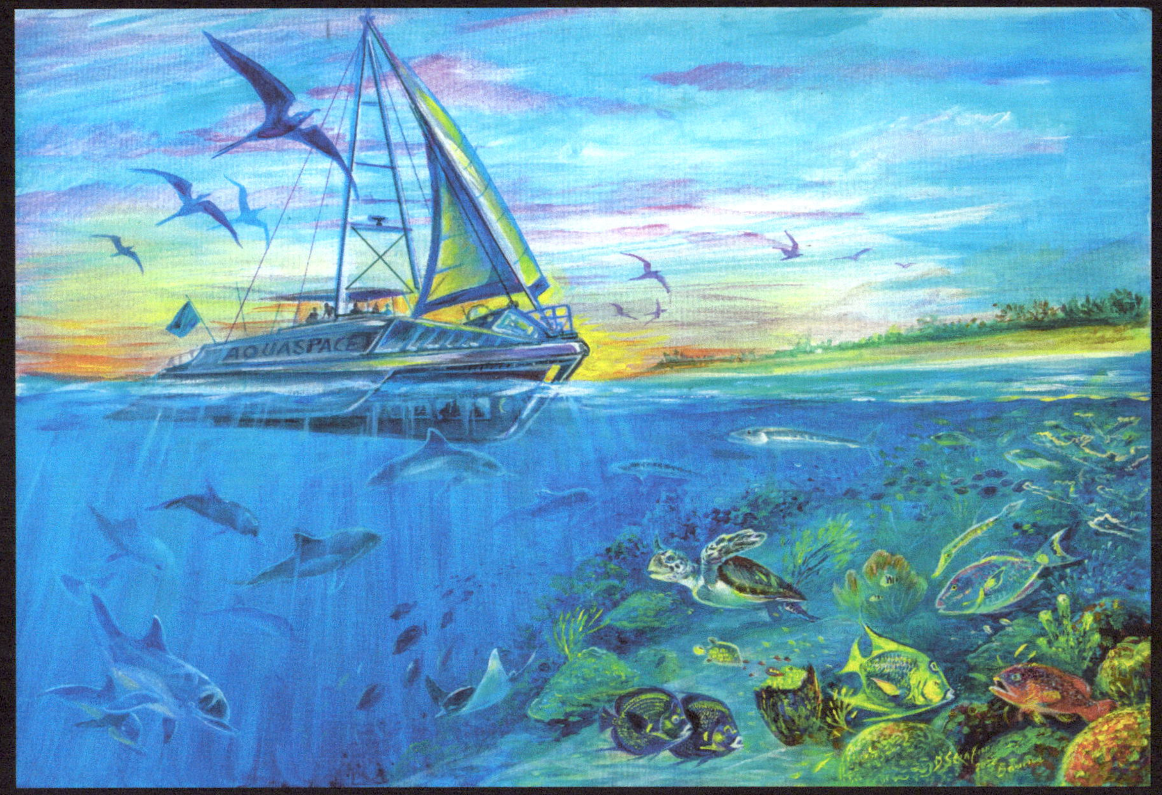

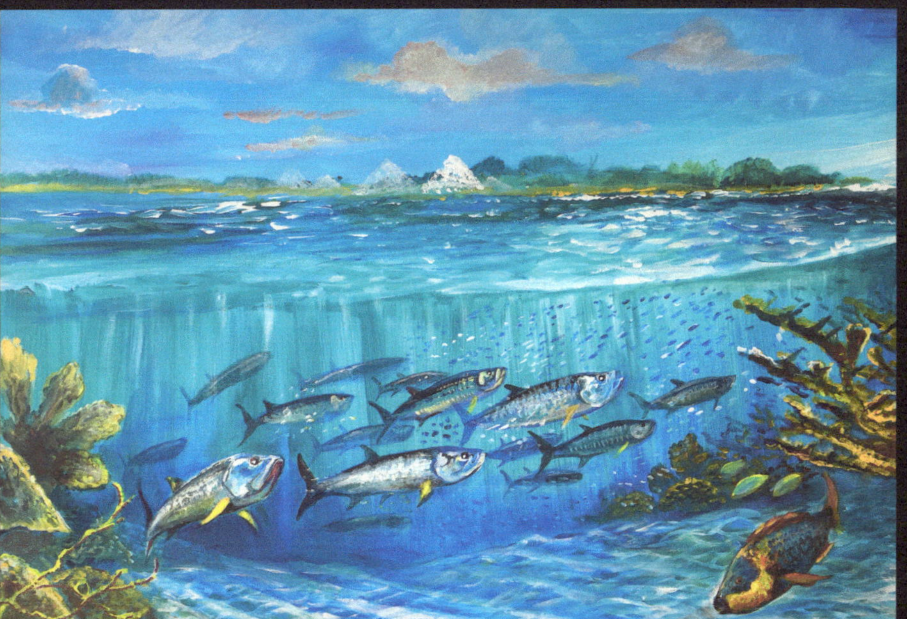

Created by French architect Jacques Rougerie, Aquaspace sails the coast of Klein Bonaire. Passengers can observe the reefs from the glass hull. On deck, they can enjoy the island's coastline and its sea birds.

Bonaire is the perfect island for observing and painting the beauty of the coral reefs. It is my underwater studio. Through this series of over-under paintings, I wanted to show how the coastline descends below the surface. This painting is of the Cai channel and its large school of tarpons.

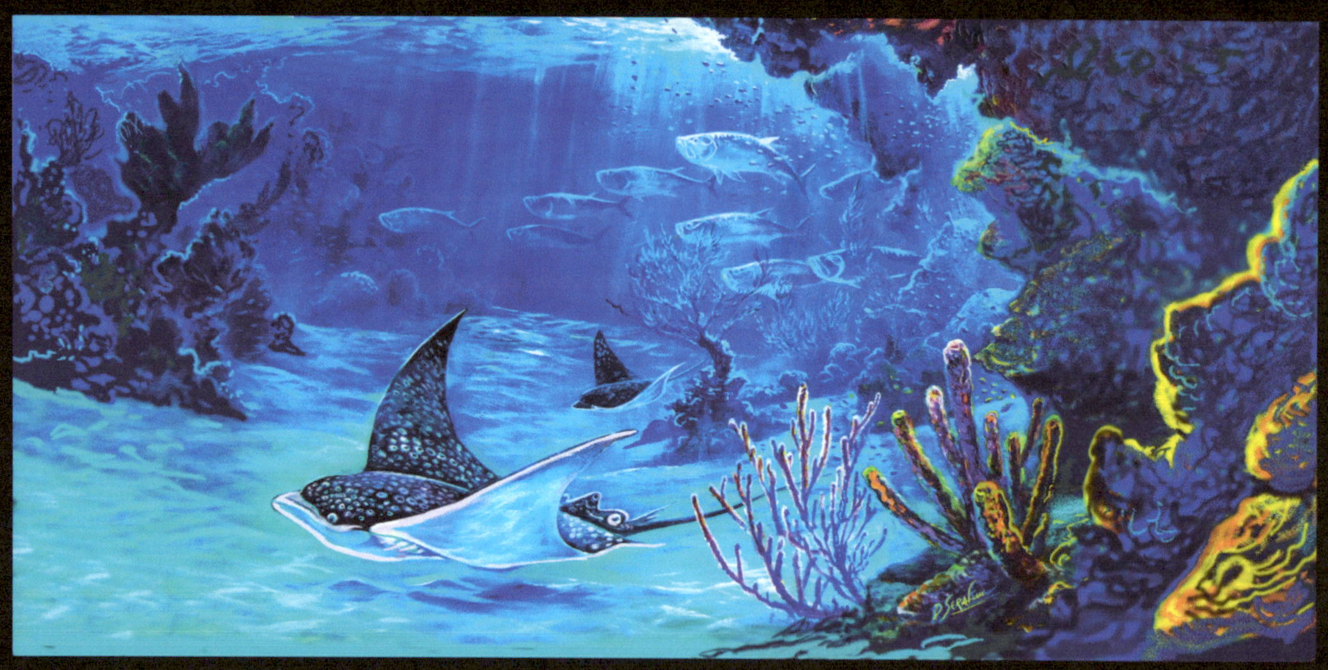

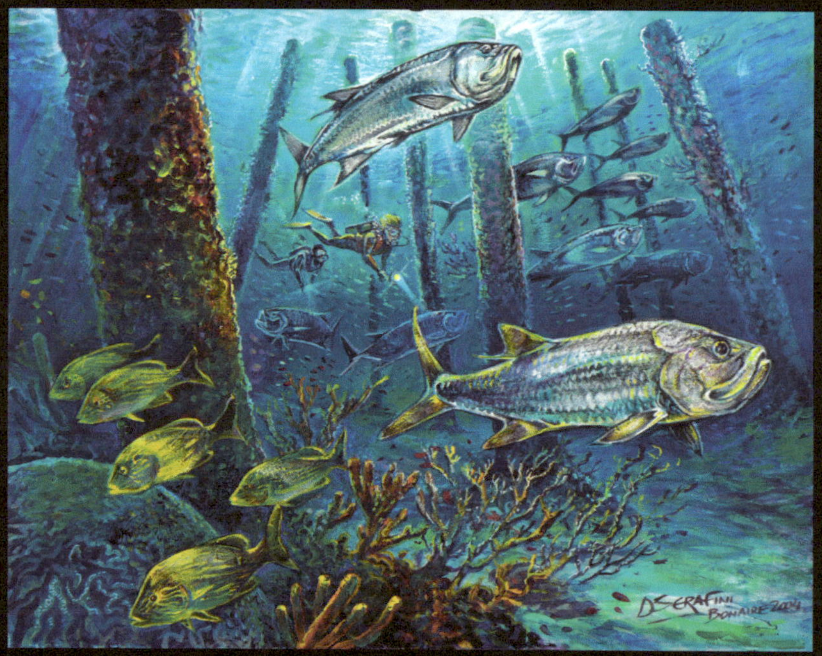

On the windward side of Bonaire is the White Hole, a sanctuary for eagle rays, turtles and tarpons. On the leeward side of Bonaire is the Salt Pier. The pilings of the pier provide shelter for hundreds of little fish, hunted by a silvery predator - tarpons.

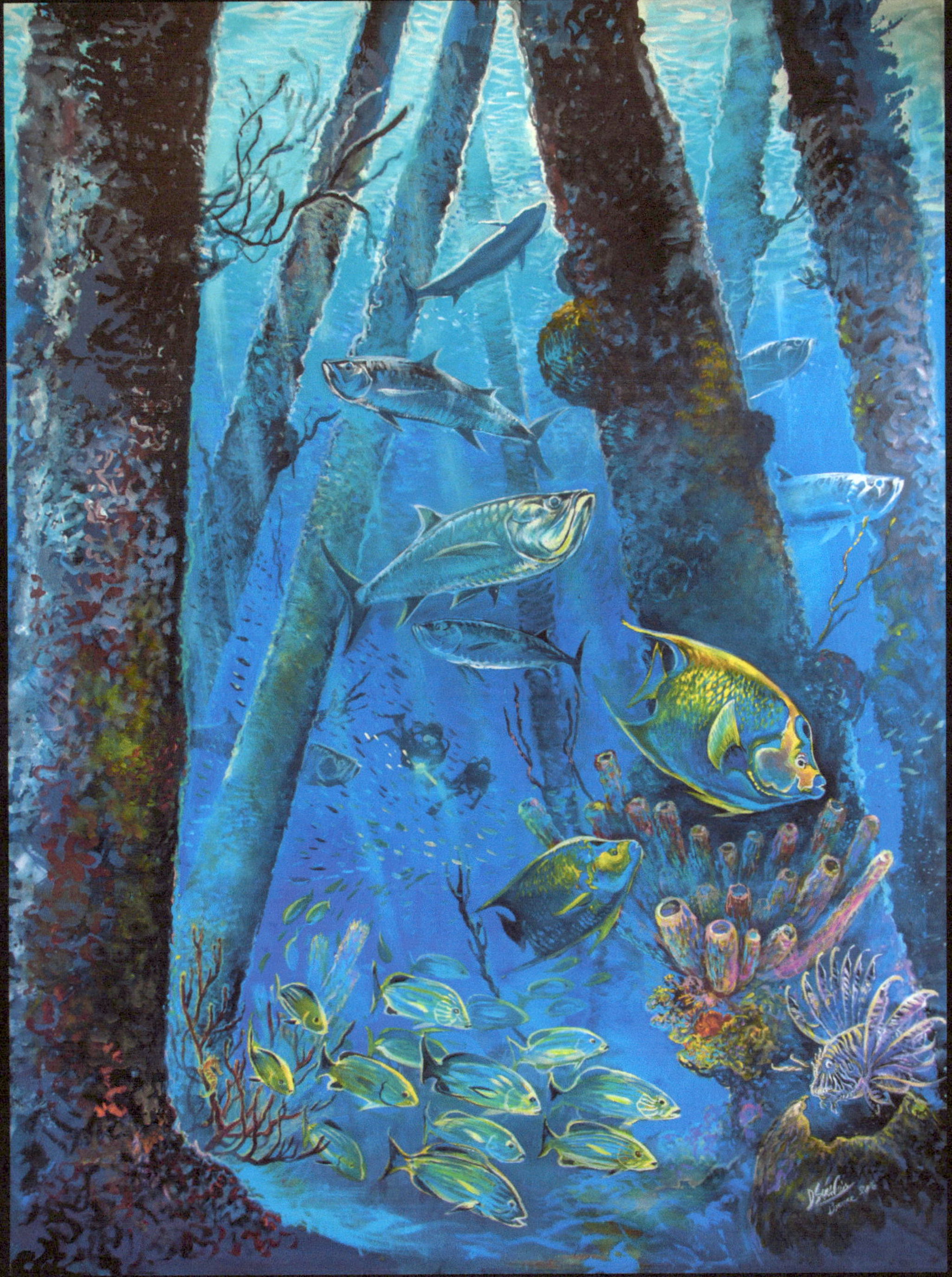

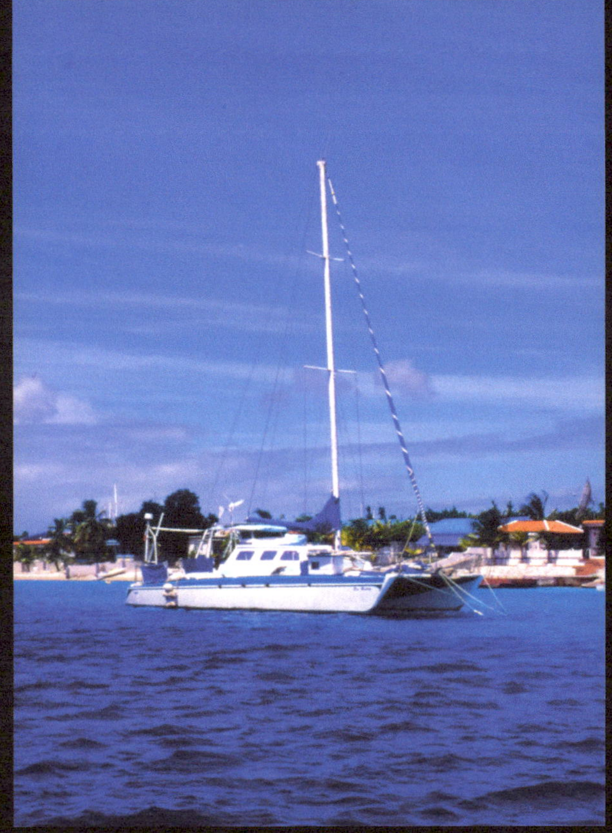

I arrived in Bonaire on board my catamaran Blue Manta. It was my floating home and my art studio for over 30 years.

The metal pilings of Salt Pier are covered with sponges and encrusting coral. Sheltering under the pier are turtles, large groups of snappers and grunts, angelfish, lionfish, barracuda and tarpons. They all seem to dance in a silent and synchronized ballet.

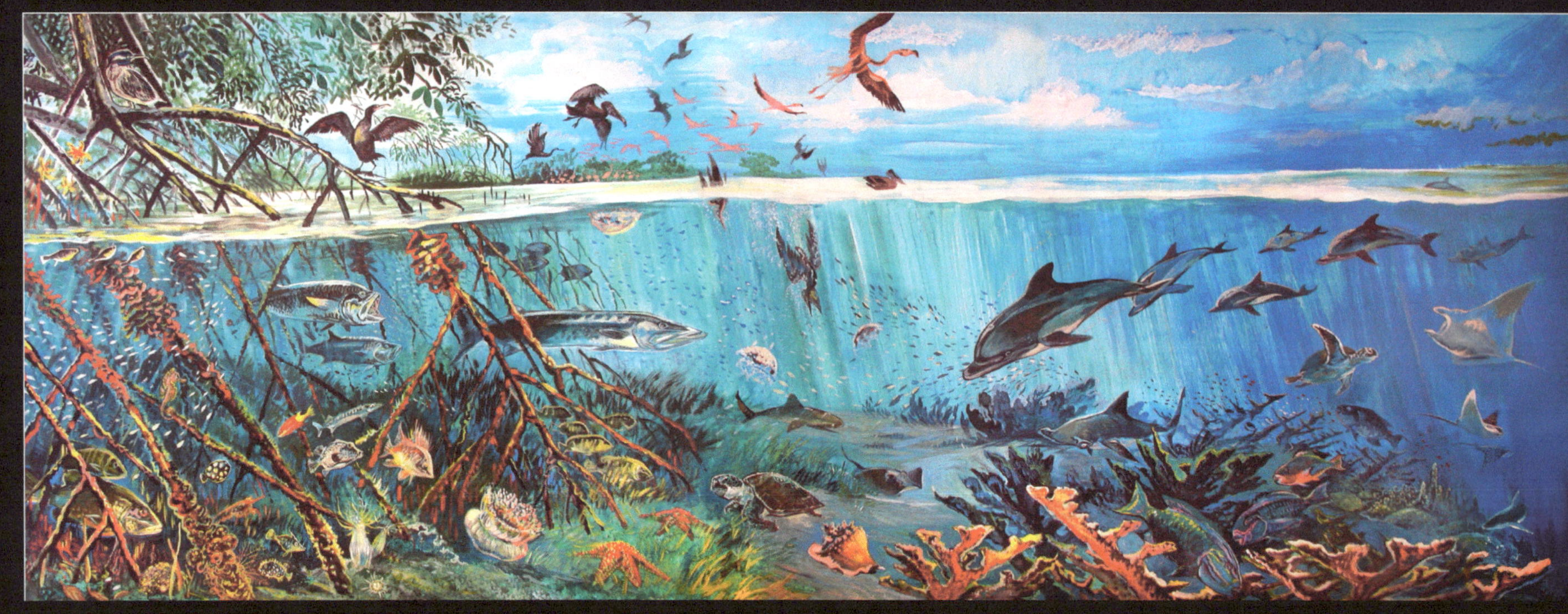

The mangroves are a nursery for juvenile fish, sharks and rays, who start their lives sheltered in the roots of the trees. Once matured they make their way across the sandy lagoon and eventually to the outer reefs... Such a source of inspiration and pleasure in the kingdom of Neptune! This painting adorns the walls of Bonaire's Mangrove Interpretive Center.

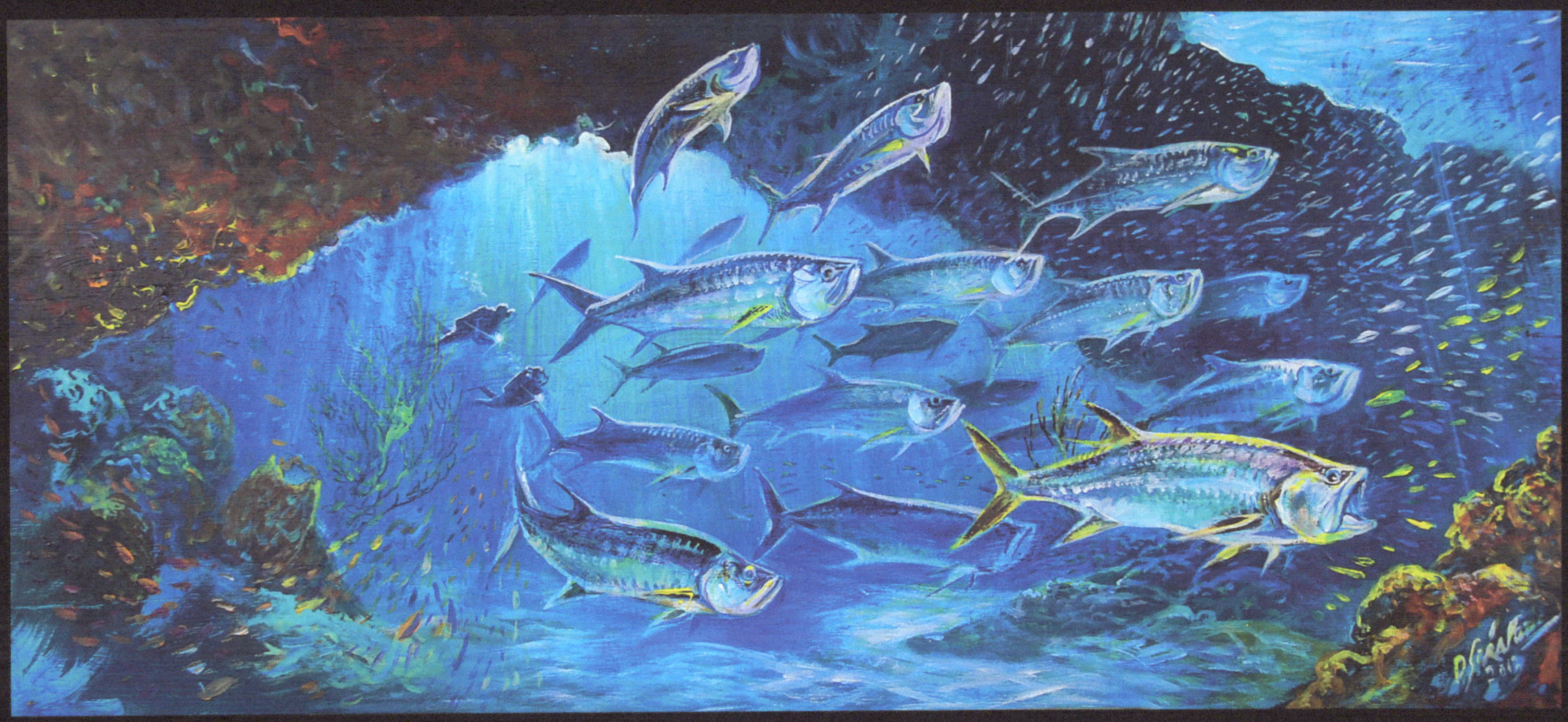

I am always on the lookout for interesting dive sites, far away, difficult to access, usually battered by waves and still unknown to other divers. That's how I discovered this great arch on the windward side of Curaçao, home to a big school of tarpons.

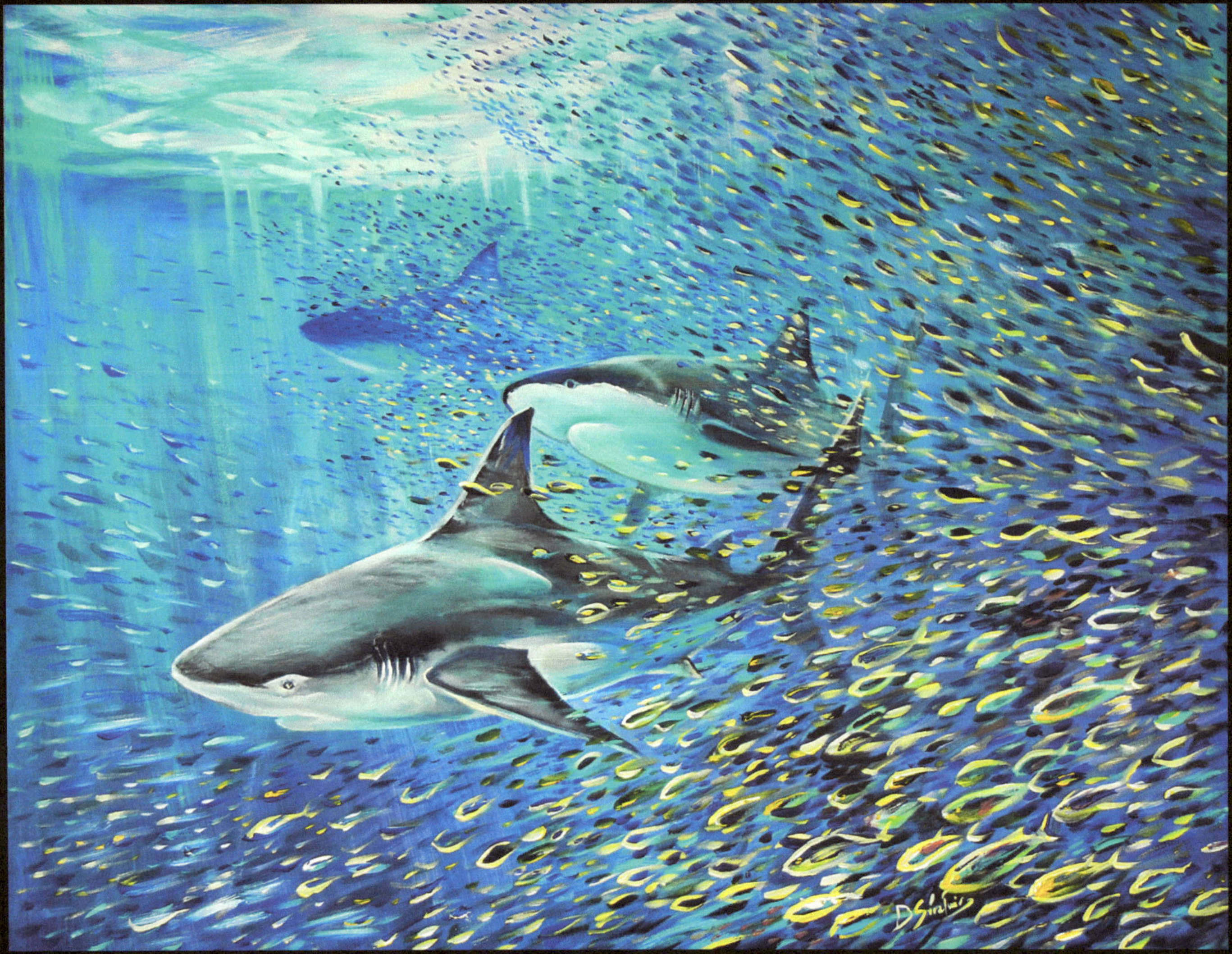

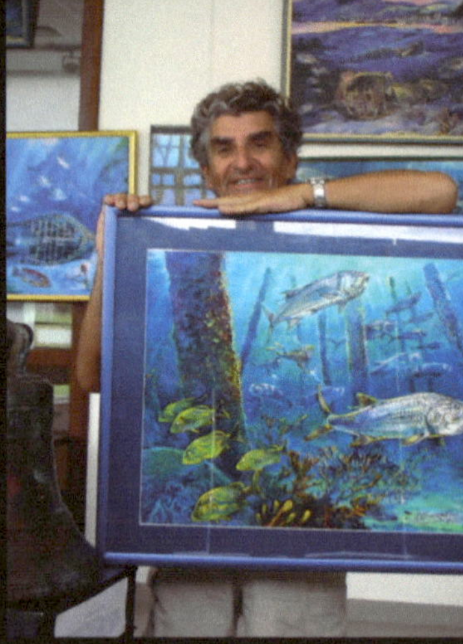

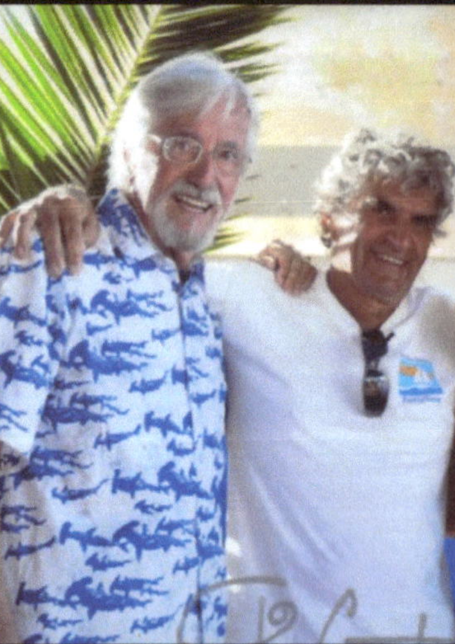

The Caribbean, the Mediterranean, the Pacific Ocean, the Indian Ocean... I've had the chance to dive with Catherine and many other diving friends, who have joined me at the four corners of our blue planet. I follow the tireless example of Jean-Michel Cousteau, now in his 80s.

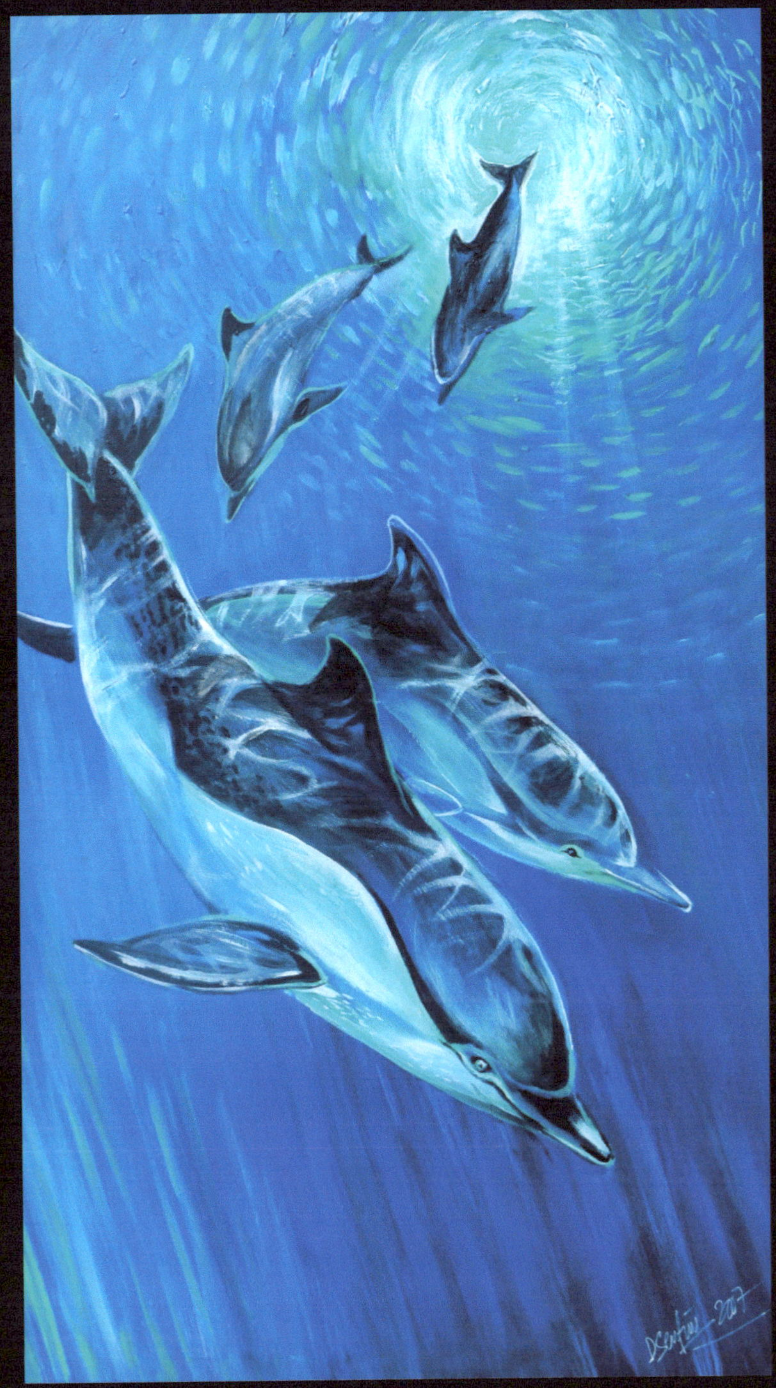

The blue waltz of dolphins.

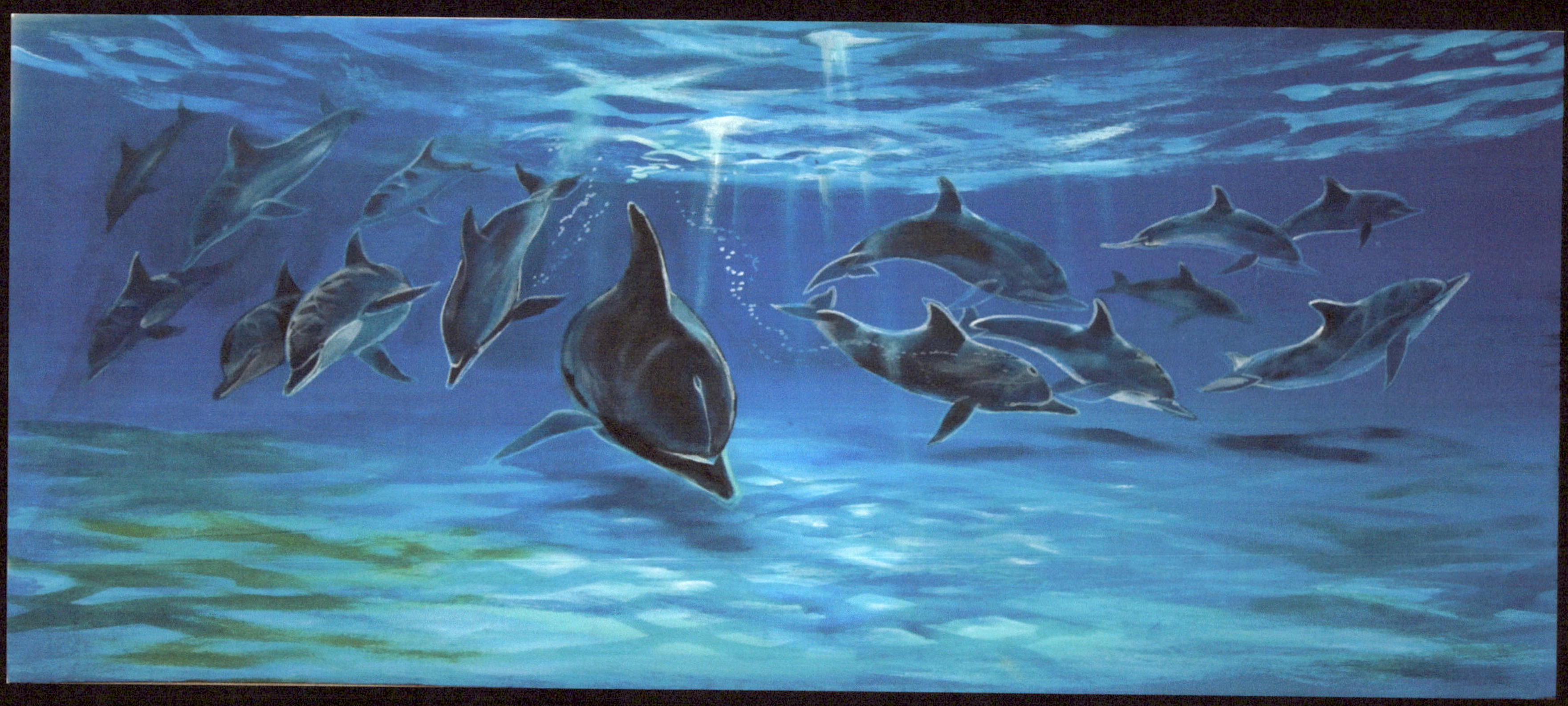

In the blue or close to a reef, they suddenly appear. They observe and once their curiosity is satisfied, they disappear once again into the blue. They are dolphins, our distant cousins that fascinate us with their grace.

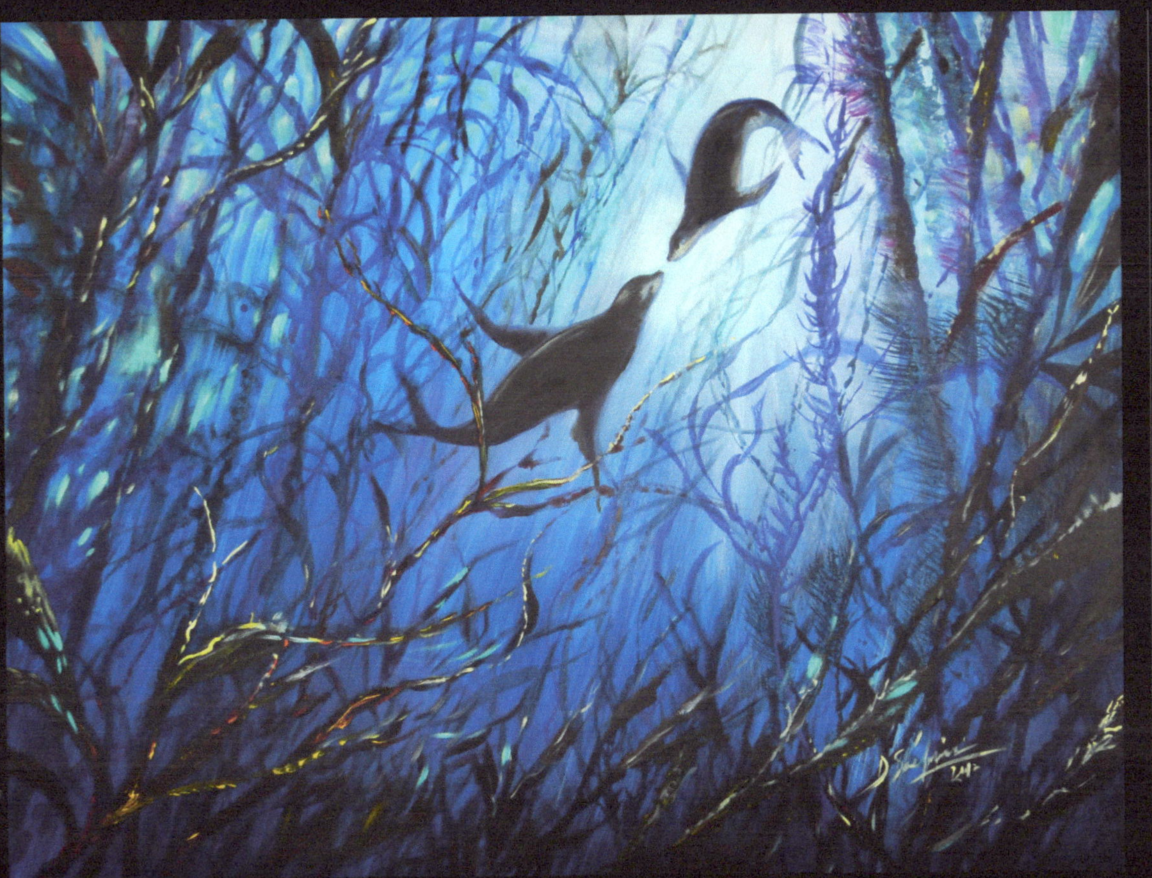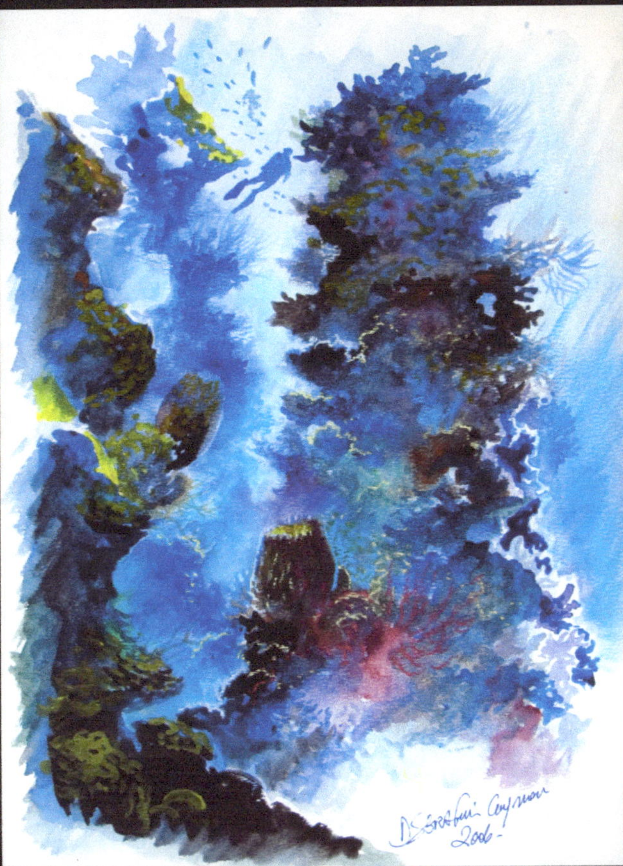

So many marvelous sites and sensations… In the California kelp forests, sea lions play. In Cayman Island and in Cozumel, we play in the complex labyrinths of coral. No, diving is not a sport. It is a weightless trip to another planet.

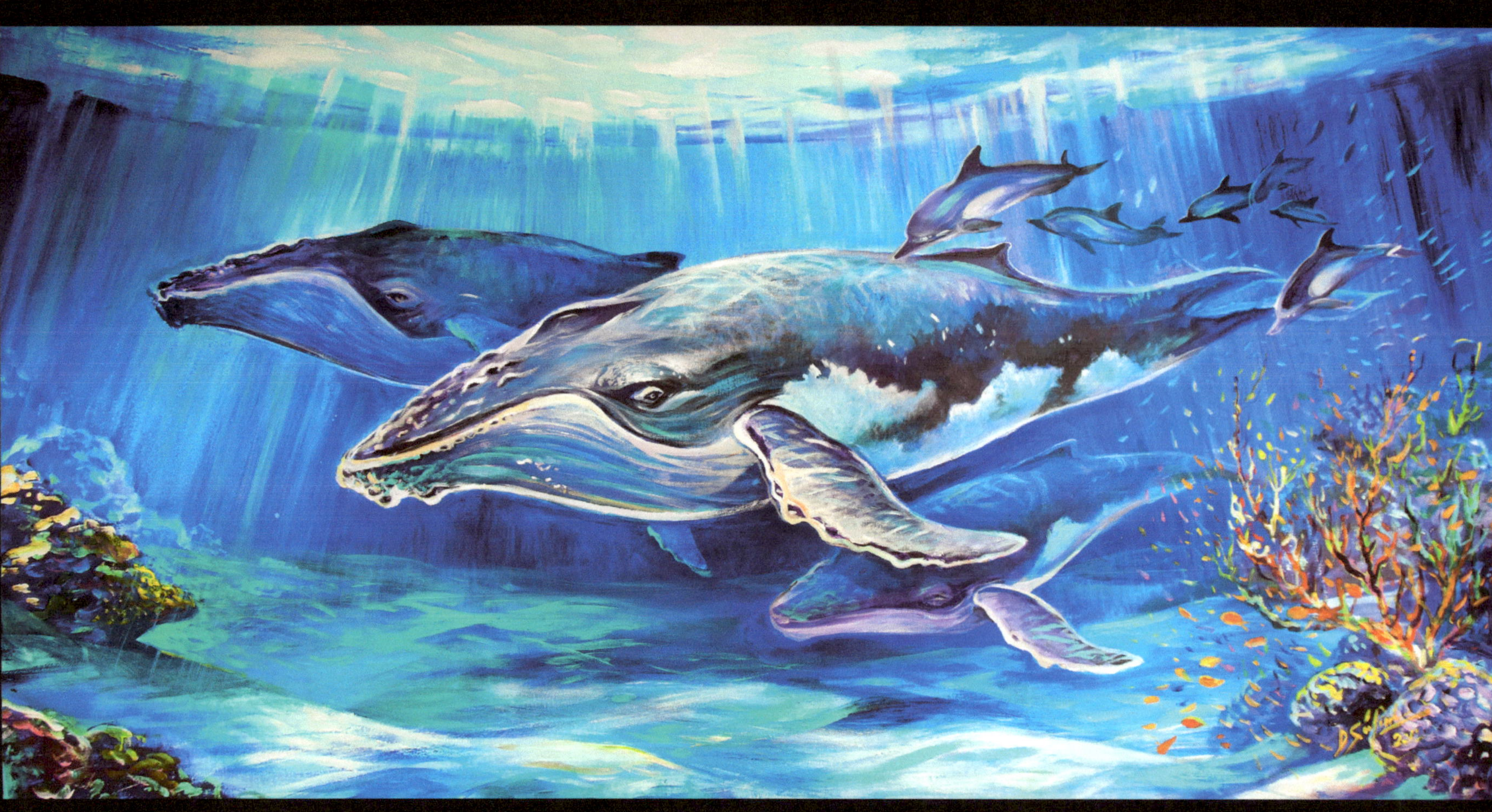

It's an unforgettable experience to exchange looks with the gentle giants of the ocean. A family of humpback whales entering a lagoon in Tonga.

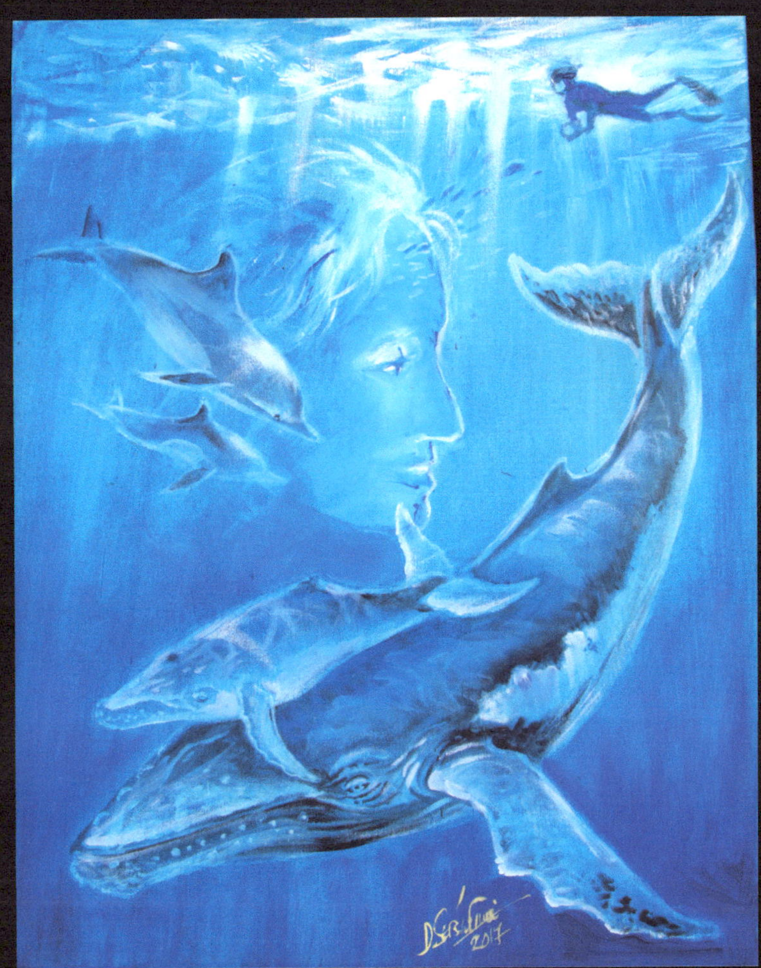

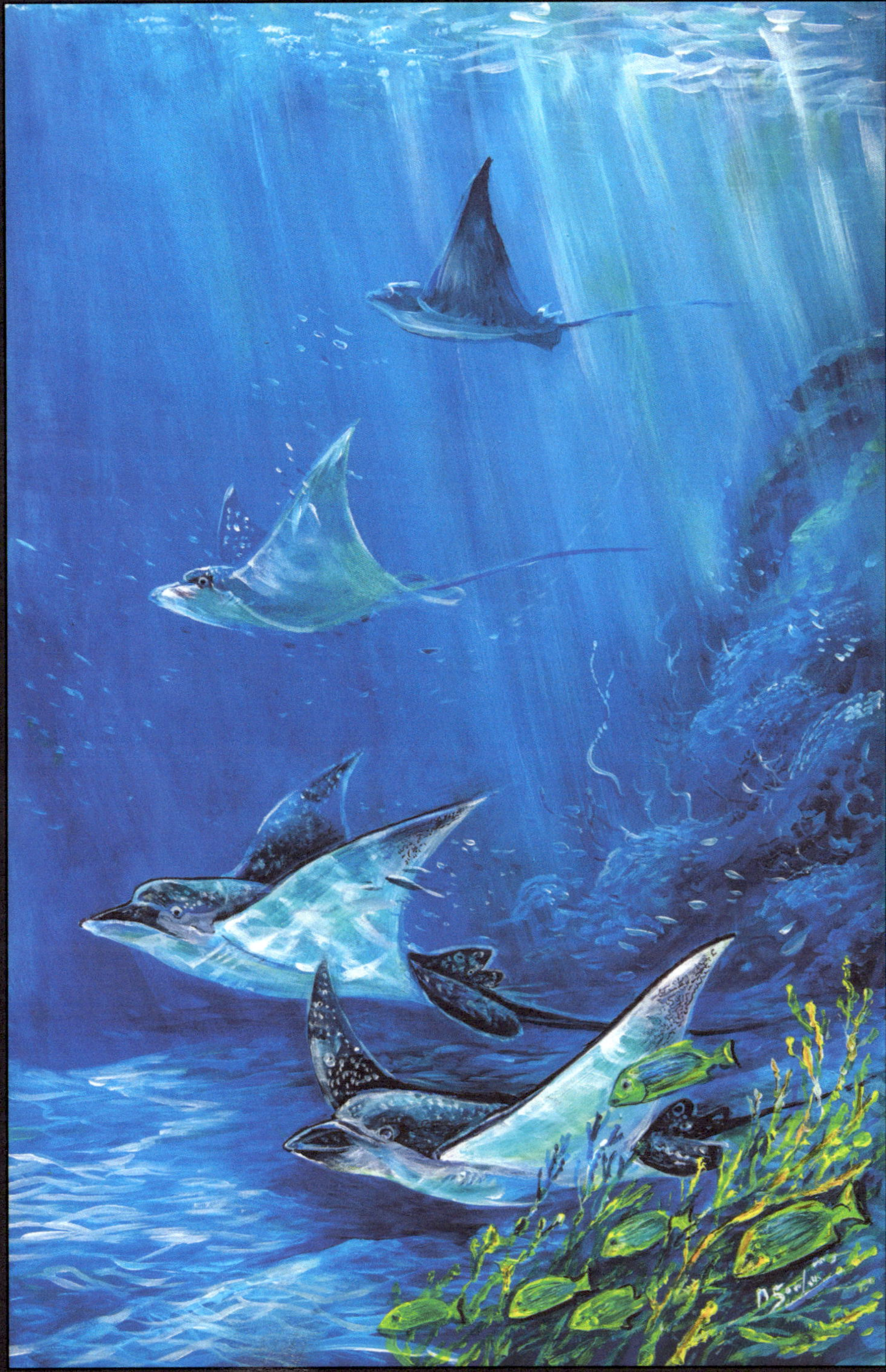

In memory of our encounter with the whales of Tonga, I created this portrait of Catherine, marking this unforgettable trip and experience. My fascination with large sea creatures not only includes whales but also these eagle rays that glide through the blue.

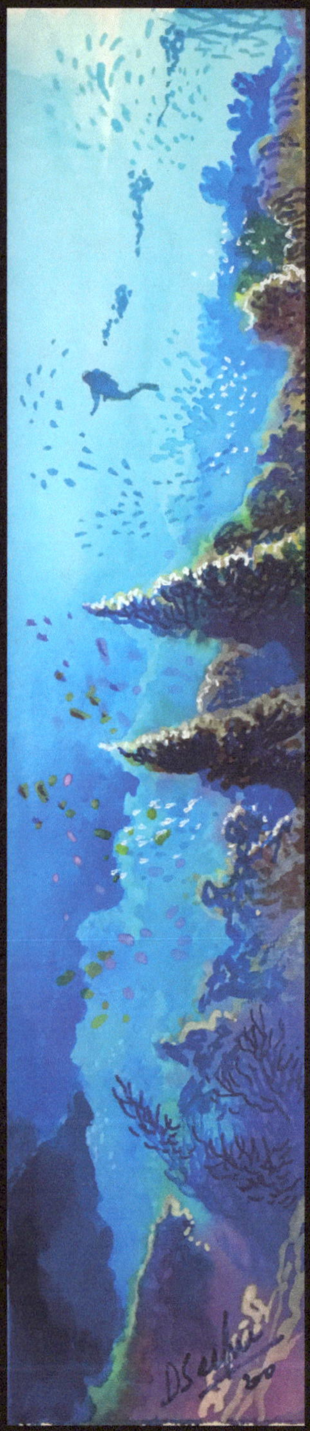

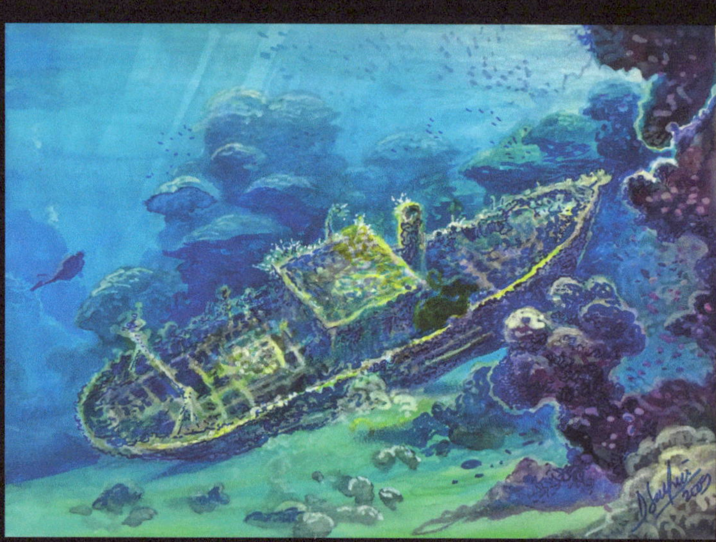

I discovered the Red Sea a long time ago. In 1970, with a
knapsack on my back full of dive equipment, sketch pads
and watercolors, I left France and hitchhiked to the Red Sea.
I still vividly remember my dives along the coast or on board
of fishing boats with local fishermen.

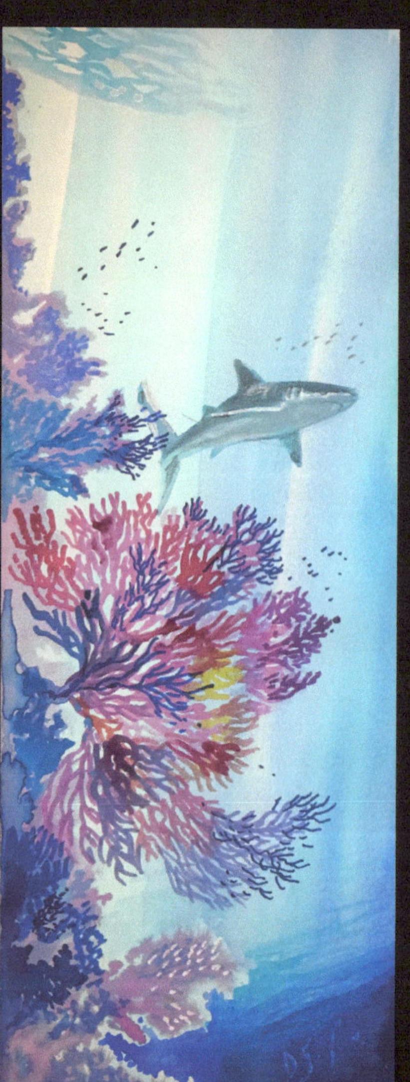

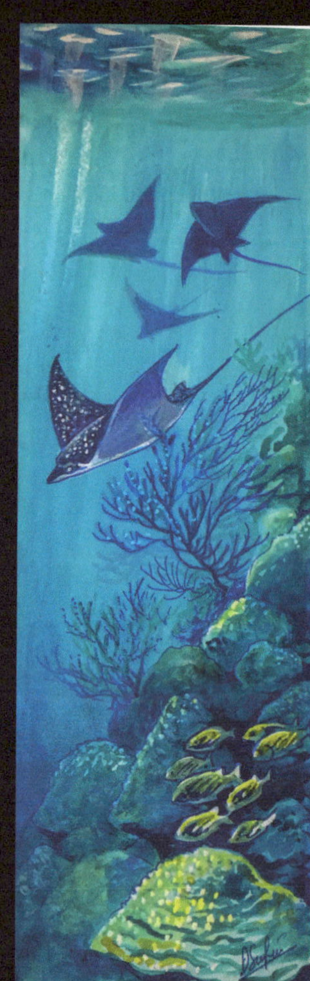

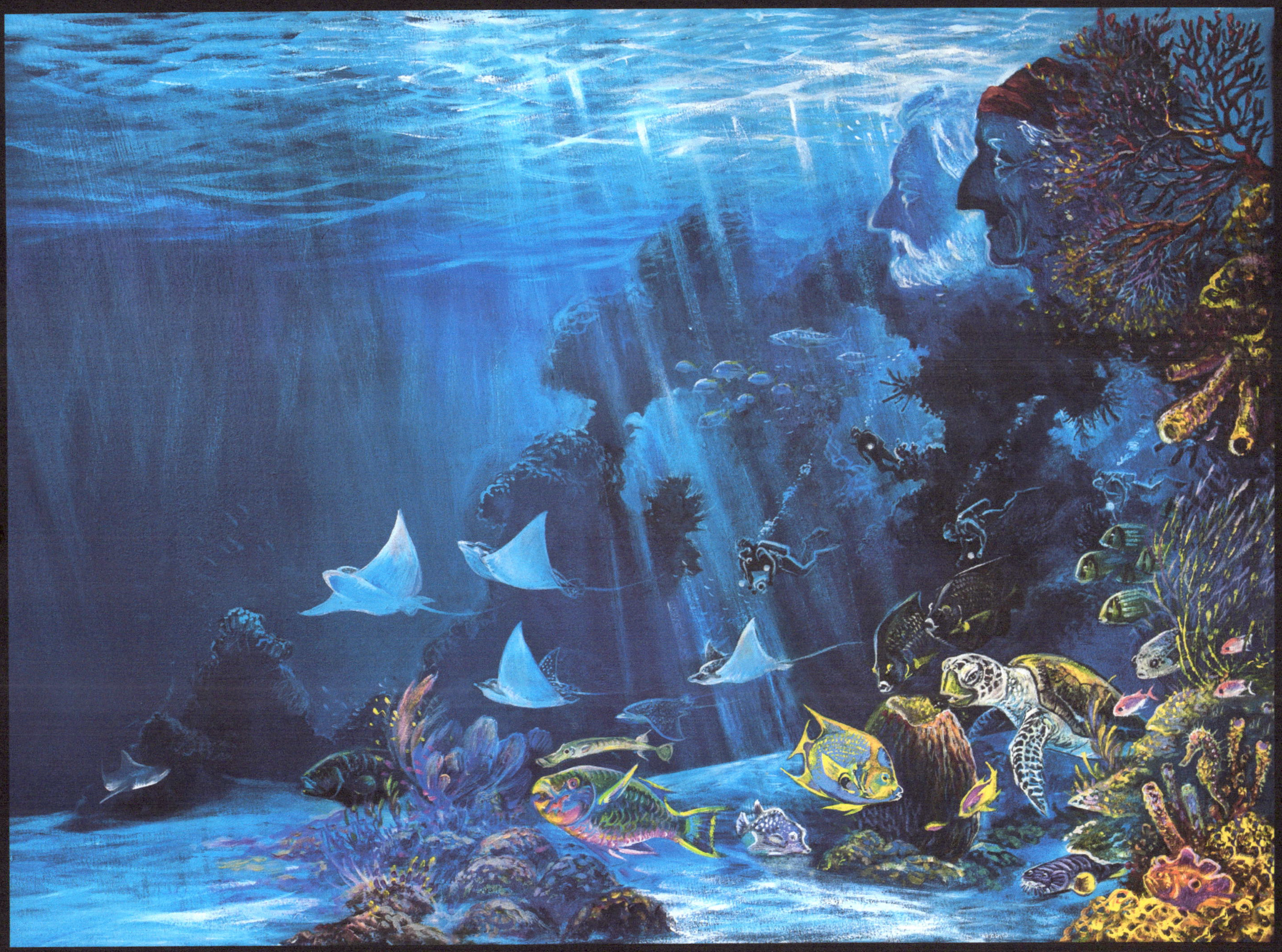

I have had the chance to discover the rich underwater world that was once ignored by humans. I hope this book has given you the desire to follow in the footsteps of Jacques-Yves Cousteau and his son Jean-Michel, who you see in my painting, keeping watch over the reef.

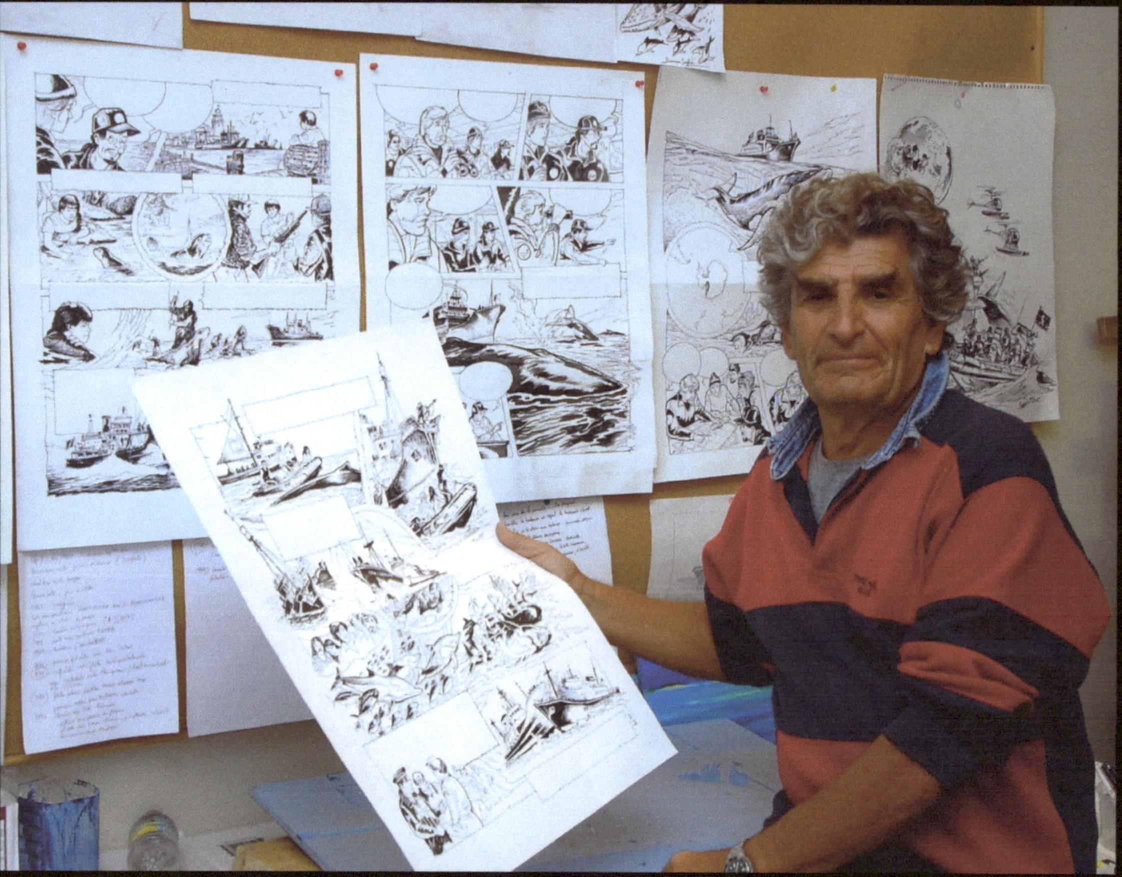

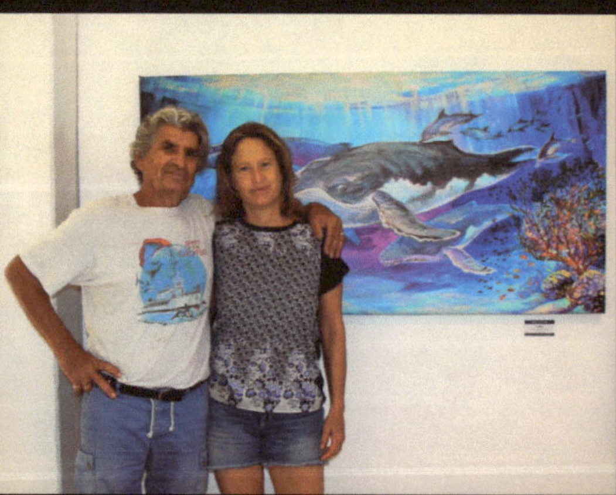

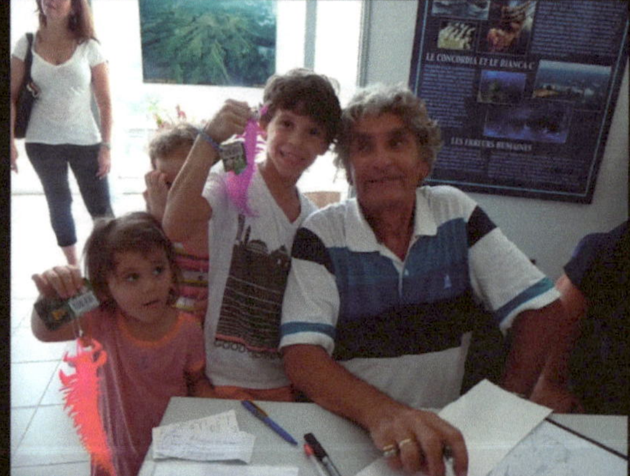

With Catherine, I continue to dive and paint. I hope that my grandchildren, Romain, Ava, Manon and Namira will discover the same wonders as we did and make some beautiful trip into the blue.

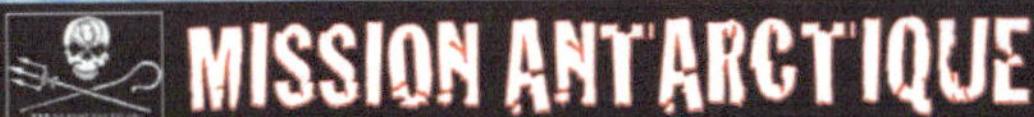

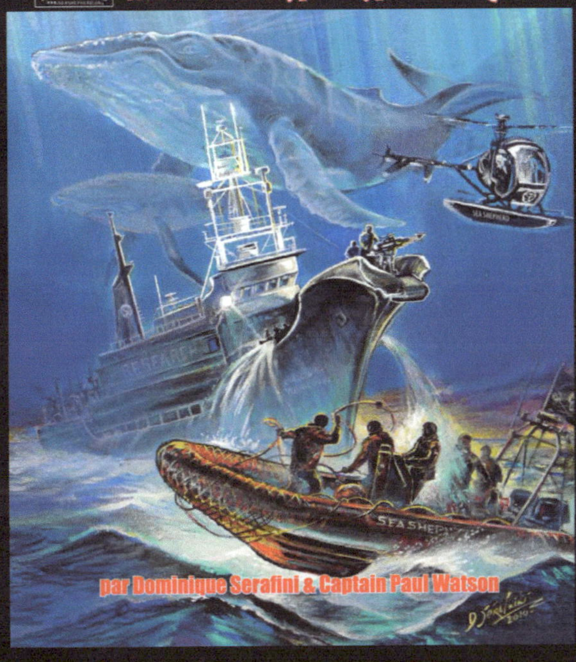

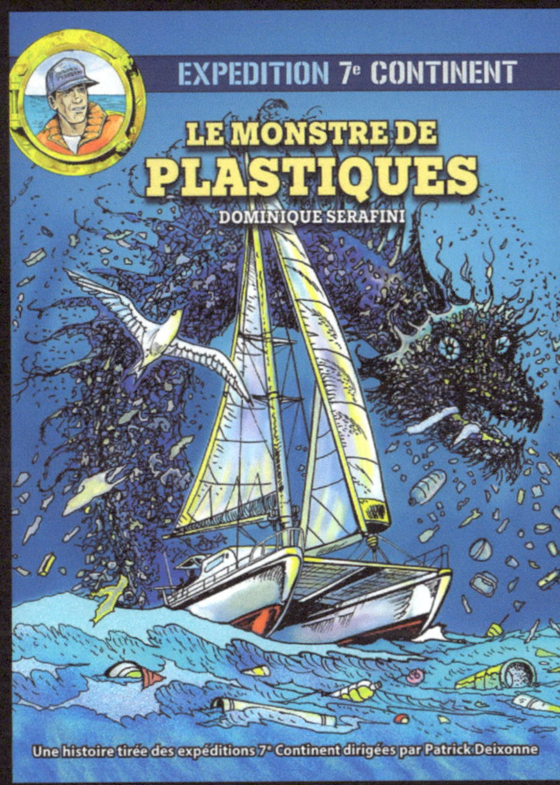

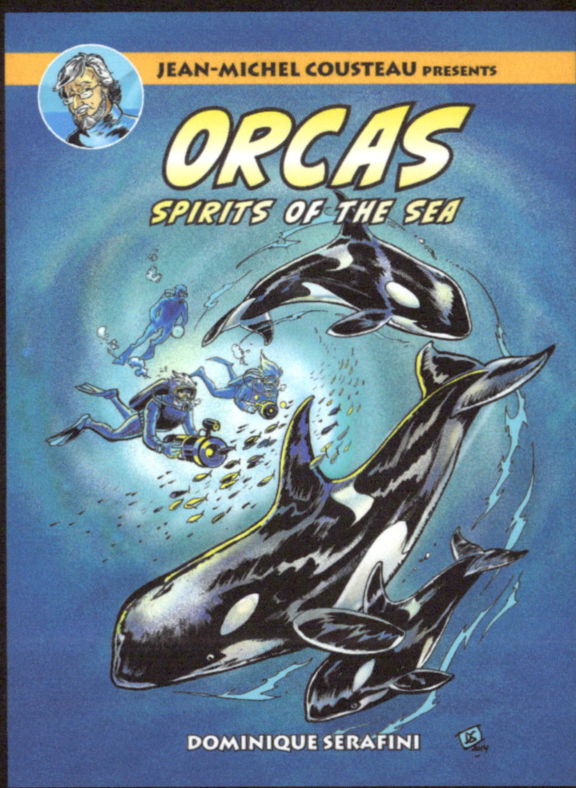

I continue to participate in the fight to defend life on our blue planet. I've created books with environmental organizations like Sea Shepherd, 7th Continent and Ocean Futures. My pencils and paint brushes are my only weapons. I communicate with young people and hope to incite them to defend our seas.

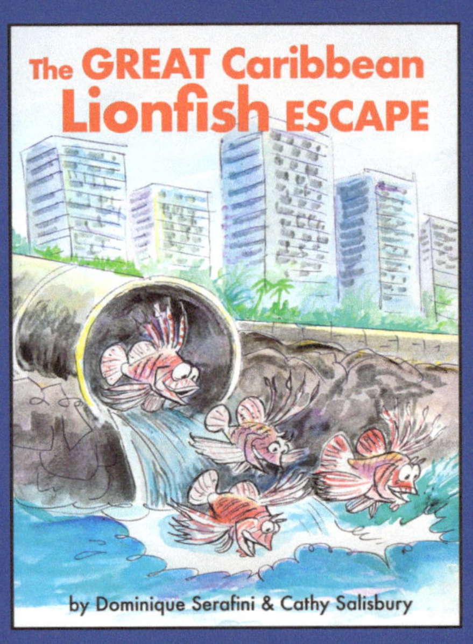

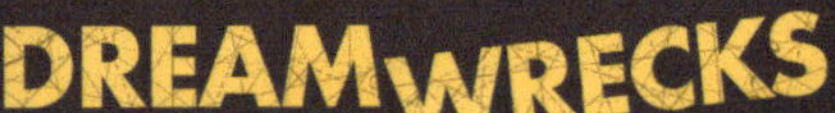

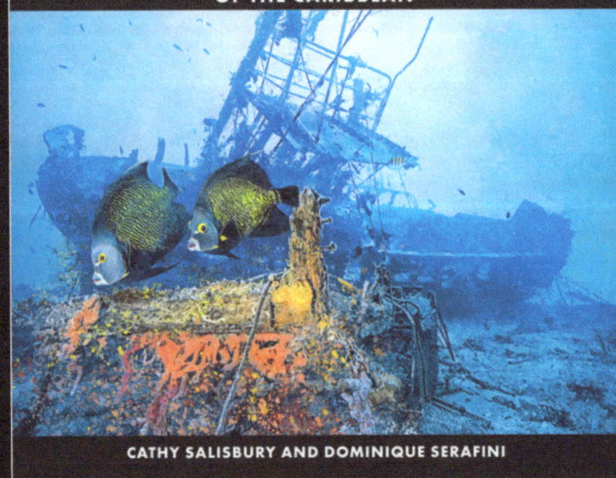

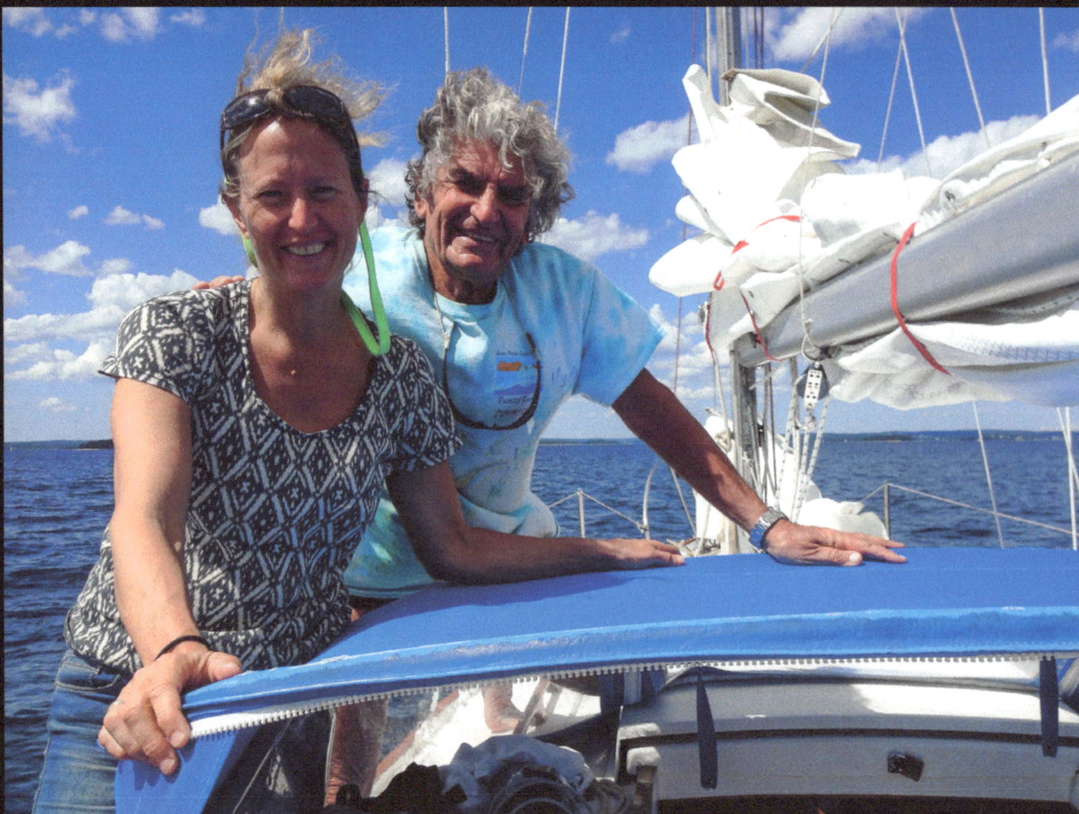

Life has many surprises in store and amongst the biggest of surprises was the day Catherine came to dive with me in Bonaire. Since then, we are together. We dive and write books to share our happiness but also our concern for the sea. The world is changing fast and the underwater world is suffering from human activities.

The arrival of the lionfish in Bonaire gave us the idea to create a book for children on this subject. The 2020 book «DreamWrecks» was inspired by our dives around the Caribbean on shipwrecks. The wrecks featured have been transformed into marine life sanctuaries. Sponges and coral cover the wounded hulls and erase the traces of the wrecks' dramatic stories.

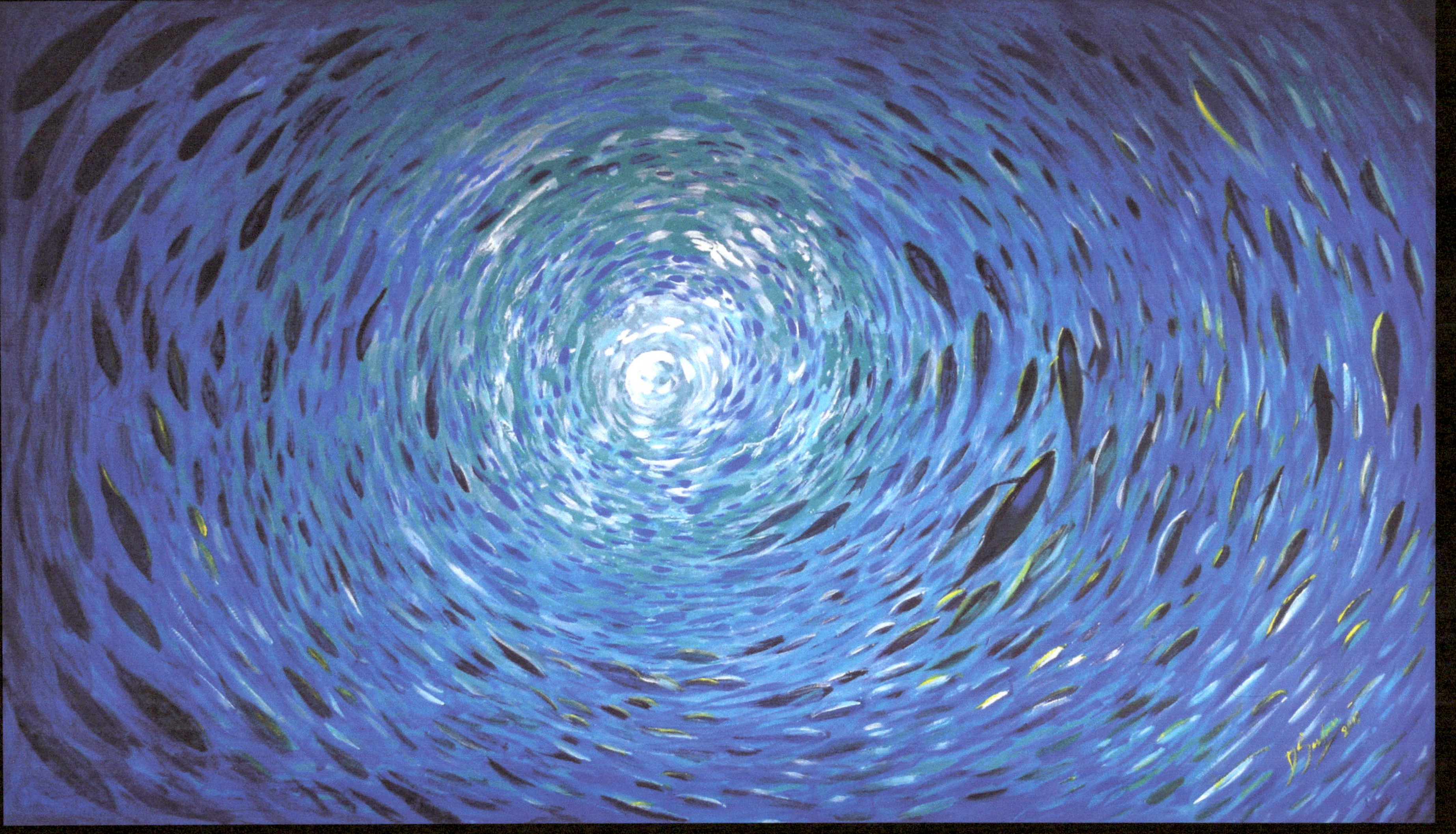

«The Whirlpool of Life». This painting is symbolic of nature's powers. From tiny planktonic creatures to giant 20-meter blue whales, all sea creatures depend on each other to survive. So, protecting life in the sea is also protecting our own lives. If the oceans survive, so then will we.

I wish you great enjoyment on our blue planet!